APR 1 7

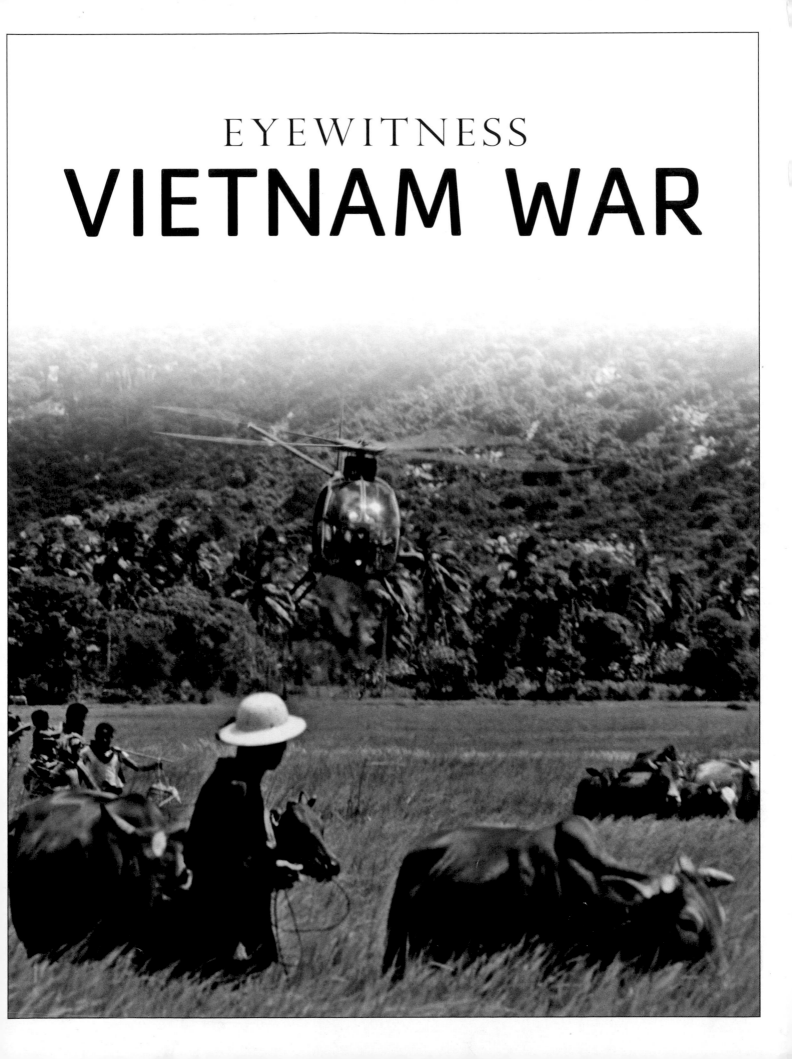

EYEWITNESS
VIETNAM WAR

VC guerrillas
demonstrate ambush

Vietminh medal
for bravery

Soviet-made 7D
grenade launcher

US lensatic
military compass

US military
dog tags

Peace-symbol
button

Chinese-made penicillin,
used by the Viet Cong

MADDOX
731

USS *Maddox* uniform patch

Montagnard
crossbow and
arrows

EYEWITNESS
VIETNAM WAR

Written by
STUART MURRAY

Lyndon B. Johnson
1964 campaign button

North Vietnamese
Air Force symbol

M-1 bayonet

Penguin
Random
House

DK PUBLISHING, INC.
Senior Editor Barbara Berger Senior Designer Tai Blanche
Additional Design Jeremy Canceko, Jee Chang, and Jessica Lasher
Assistant Managing Art Editor Michelle Baxter
Creative Director Tina Vaughan Jacket Art Director Dirk Kaufman
Production Manager Ivor Parker DTP Coordinator Milos Orlovic

MEDIA PROJECTS, INC.
Executive Editor Carter Smith Project Editor Aaron R. Murray
Associate Editor Margaret C. F. McLaughlin
Production Manager James A. Burmester
Consultants Clifford J. Rogers and Steve R. Waddell, United States Military Academy
Cartography Ron Toelke, Rob Stokes Picture Researcher Erika Rubel
Copy Editor Glenn Novak

RELAUNCH EDITION
DK US
Senior Editor Margaret Parrish Editorial Director Nancy Ellwood

DK INDIA
Editors Deeksha Saikia, Antara Raghavan Assistant Art Editor Nidhi Rastogi
DTP Designer Pawan Kumar Senior DTP Designer Harish Aggarwal
Picture Researcher Sakshi Saluja Jacket Designer Garima Sharma
Managing Editor Kingshuk Ghoshal Managing Art Editor Govind Mittal

DK UK
Senior Art Editor Spencer Holbrook Jacket Editor Claire Gell
Jackets Design Development Manager Sophia MTT
Producer, pre-production Jacqueline Street Producer Gary Batchelor
Managing Editor Francesca Baines Managing Art Editor Philip Letsu
Publisher Andrew Macintyre Associate Publishing Director Liz Wheeler
Art Director Karen Self Design Director Phil Ormerod
Publishing Director Jonathan Metcalf

Consultant Professor David Anderson

First American Edition, 2005
This edition published in the United States in 2017 by
DK Publishing, 345 Hudson Street, New York, New York 10014

Copyright © 2005, 2017 Dorling Kindersley Limited

DK, a Division of Penguin Random House LLC
17 18 19 20 21 10 9 8 7 6 5 4 3 2 1
001–305108–January/2017

A catalog record for this book is available from the Library of Congress.
ISBN: 978-1-4654-5984-8 (Paperback)
ISBN: 978-1-4654-5985-5 (ALB)

DK books are available at special discounts when purchased in bulk for sales
promotions, premiums, fund-raising, or educational use. For details, contact:
DK Publishing Special Markets, 345 Hudson Street, New York, New York 10014
SpecialSales@dk.com

Printed and bound in Hong Kong

A WORLD OF IDEAS:
SEE ALL THERE IS TO KNOW

www.dk.com

North
Vietnamese
stamp

AN/PRC-25
backpack field radio

US infantry helmet

South Vietnamese
200-dong note, 1966

Soviet-made
antitank land mine

Chinese cobra

Contents

US M-16A1
assault rifle

Indochina War

Stamp
France issued postage stamps for its colonies in Indochina, such as this one from 1907.

The destruction of World War II weakened France's colonial empire. During the war, Japan took control of French colonies in Indochina. In 1945, Vietnamese nationalists, led by Ho Chi Minh, a Communist, battled Japanese forces for independence. Known as the Vietminh, they worked with US agents against Japan. After Japan's defeat, Ho declared Vietnam independent, but the French refused to recognize Vietnam.

Emperor Bao Dai
European-educated Bao Dai, above with French officials in the 1920s, was the 13th and last emperor of Vietnam. Vietnamese nationalists considered him a puppet of France.

Vietnamese dragon

Bao Dai stamp

Japanese "Rising Sun" battle flag

Japanese warships
Japan's battleships patrol the waters as troops on land fight the Vietminh. Ho Chi Minh's army gained valuable experience fighting the Japanese.

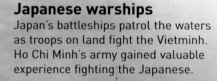

Vietminh training
A US military adviser observes Vietminh fighters practicing grenade-throwing. The Vietminh included Communist and non-Communist nationalists. After the war, Ho Chi Minh won support from Communist China and the Soviet Union.

Map of Vietnam

Portrait of Ho Chi Minh

Early currency of the Democratic Republic of Vietnam (DRV)

French military parade

French soldiers in Hanoi drive past cheering French colonial residents and Vietnamese supporters. France tried to retake control in Indochina after World War II. Some Vietnamese favored French rule. Many French-allied Vietnamese were educated in Europe and had converted to Catholicism.

Independence

Ho Chi Minh speaks to Vietnamese nationalists in Hanoi on September 2, 1945, the day of Japan's surrender. Ho declared an independent Democratic Republic of Vietnam (DRV). The French initially granted limited freedoms to the DRV, but clashes followed. As hostility between the DRV and France made war unavoidable, the US backed France.

Truman and Acheson

President Harry S. Truman, left, meets with Secretary of State Dean Acheson. Both believed that if Vietnam were ruled by Ho's Communists, other countries in the region would also become Communist. Acheson persuaded Truman to give France aid to oppose the Communists.

INDOCHINA TIMELINE

1940   Japan takes over French Indochina.
1941   Ho Chi Minh establishes the Vietminh, the "League for the Independence of Vietnam."
1945   Japan surrenders. Ho Chi Minh forms the Democratic Republic of Vietnam (DRV).
1946   French troops clash with DRV forces, sparking the First Indochina War.
1950   French suffer defeats; US sets up the Military Assistance Advisory Group (MAAG).
1951   France controls cities, Vietminhn, countryside.
1954   Vietminh take Dien Pien Phu and defeat French, ending First Indochina War. Treaty divides Vietnam into North and South.

France loses Indochina

Early in the First Indochina War, American military supplies gave the French an advantage over the Vietminh. The French captured the cities, but Ho Chi Minh and General Vo Nguyen Giap would not accept defeat. They reorganized the army in the jungles and mountains and took aid from Communist China. In late 1953, the French built a base in the mountains at Dien Bien Phu. By spring, Colonel Christian de Castries and 15,000 troops were surrounded there by Giap's 55,000 men. After a 55-day siege, de Castries surrendered in May 1954. The Vietminh prepared for an independent Vietnam.

Canteen

Parachuting in

French paratroopers land at Dien Bien Phu in late 1953 to establish a new base. By spring, Vietminh artillery had destroyed the French airfield, and ground attacks were capturing French positions.

Impossible odds

In a bunker at Dien Bien Phu, Colonel de Castries faces surrender or death. His force was cut off from help and under heavy bombardment. He was taken prisoner, but survived captivity.

Sandbags protect walls

US military gear used by the French

French defeat

Ho Chi Minh, left, studies the layout of Dien Bien Phu, a French base on the Laos border. General Vo Nguyen Giap, right, commanded the Vietminh forces. The French won several clashes during the war, but, in the end, Giap and Ho were better strategists.

Soldier's bundled bedding and coat

Doomed defenders

Weary French troops fought bravely for nearly two months. They did not expect the Vietminh to drag cannon up the mountains and bombard their base. About 2,000 French troops and 8,000 Vietminh died, with 10,800 French captured—most of whom died of hunger and disease.

Decisive defeat

Victorious Vietnamese fighters raise their flag over Colonel de Castries's bunker. The command center fell to the Vietminh on May 7, 1954. Seven weeks later, a French armored battalion (Groupement Mobile 100) was ambushed and almost completely destroyed by the Vietminh. This decisive defeat, combined with the fall of Dien Bien Phu, ended the First Indochina War.

Communist flag

The Geneva Accords

The French and Vietminh signed peace terms in Geneva, Switzerland. Called the Geneva Accords, they granted the Communists control of Vietnam north of the 17th parallel. A non-Communist government ruled South Vietnam. Elections were to be held within two years. The United States opposed a Communist-led Vietnam and refused to accept the terms or an election.

Rubble from artillery bombardment

General Henri Delteil

North Vietnam

17th parallel

South Vietnam

Value of stamp

Communist star

Indochina truce

Former French general Henri Delteil signs truce documents on July 20, 1954, ending hostilities. A European official and Vietnamese delegates look on in Geneva's Palace of Nations.

Divided Vietnam

This North Vietnamese stamp shows North and South Vietnam separated by a line at the 17th parallel. The former French colonies Laos and Cambodia are to the left.

Vietminh medal for bravery

Victory parade

In October 1954, triumphant Vietminh troops are cheered by crowds in Hanoi. French forces had recently left for South Vietnam. After nearly eight years of war, the city was now under Vietminh control. Hanoi became North Vietnam's capital.

DIEN BIEN PHU TO ARMISTICE

- **1953** French troops number 90,000, with 100,000 Vietnamese National Army (colonial) troops; 200,000 Vietminh forces.
- **November 1953** Base built at Dien Bien Phu.
- **December 1953** French troops sent to base.
- **February 1954** Giap surrounds base.
- **March 13, 1954** Ground assaults begin.
- **May 1, 1954** Final ground attacks start.
- **May 7, 1954** Dien Bien Phu falls.
- **June 24–July 17, 1954** A 3,000-strong armored unit is wiped out.
- **August 1, 1954** Armistice.

US advisers

In 1955, President Dwight D. Eisenhower sent military advisers to the Republic of (South) Vietnam (RVN). The US helped anti-Communist Ngo Dinh Diem take power in a corrupt election. South Vietnamese Communists—the Viet Cong (VC)—armed to fight Diem's government. National Liberation Front (NLF) forces fought in the North; VC guerrillas fought in the South. Once elected president, John F. Kennedy (JFK) increased American involvement. In late 1963, both Diem and Kennedy were assassinated.

Fleeing
Refugees from northern Vietnam rush southward in 1954 to escape Hanoi's new Communist government.

First president
Diem speaks at his 1955 inauguration. A Roman Catholic, he favored other Catholics, even though 80 percent of Vietnam was Buddhist.

19th-century hero Nguyen Hué

South Vietnamese 200-dong note, 1966

Grenade launcher

US Army-issue helmet

Jungle waters
US advisers and troops from the Army of the Republic of Vietnam (ARVN) cross a river—by 1963, 14,000 US advisers were serving.

Sacks of personal possessions

An angry protest
Buddhist protesters in Saigon struggle with police at a demonstration against Diem in 1963. They objected to persecution of their religion and called for peaceful negotiations with the Communists.

10

JFK'S war
President Kennedy speaks about the threat of Communist power in Southeast Asia in 1961. During his presidency, more than $500 million in military aid flowed each year to South Vietnam, even though JFK's administration disliked Diem's corrupt government.

Battle plan
Colonel John Paul Vann, left, reviews a map with ARVN and US officers. Vann was a key figure in the US Military Assistance Advisory Group (MAAG), which oversaw advisers. He objected to the careless use of firepower and preferred winning over the people.

Laos

Communist regions of Laos are shaded

MAAG uniform patch

Conspirators
Ambitious ARVN generals led by Duong Van Minh, near right, murdered President Diem on November 1, 1963, and took power. They, too, were soon overthrown. As US involvement increased, the republic was rocked by military coups (overthrows).

Kennedy assassination
President and Mrs. Kennedy were riding in a motorcade through Dallas on November 22, 1963, when he was shot by a sniper. Vice President Lyndon B. Johnson, below, took the oath of office with Mrs. Kennedy at his side.

JFK's limousine

CHICAGO DAILY NEWS

PRESIDENT IS KILLED
Texas Sniper Escapes; Johnson Sworn In

Story Begins on Next Page

Chicago Daily News front page coverage of JFK's assassination

THE MAIN PLAYERS

- **ARVN** Army of the Republic of (South) Vietnam.
- **RVN** Republic of (South) Vietnam.
- **DRV** Democratic Republic of (North) Vietnam.
- **NLF** National Liberation Front, founded in 1960.
- **MAAG** Military Assistance Advisory Group, formed by US in 1950 to aid France. Replaced by **MACV** (Military Assistance Command, Vietnam) in 1962.

Gulf of Tonkin

In the summer of 1964, the US destroyer *Maddox* was in the Gulf of Tonkin, near North Vietnam, gathering information about enemy naval bases. On August 2, the *Maddox* was fired on by torpedo boats. It returned fire, sinking one boat. Commander Herbert L. Ogier's report went to President Lyndon B. Johnson (LBJ). Two nights later, electronics operators thought another attack was underway, and LBJ ordered airstrikes. On August 7, Congress passed the Gulf of Tonkin Resolution, giving the president broad war powers. The *Maddox* crew had been mistaken about the second attack, but LBJ was now committed to waging war against the Communist Vietnamese.

Map labels:
- CHINA
- NORTH VIETNAM
- Hòn Gai
- Hanoi
- Haiphong
- LAOS
- Thanh Hoa
- NVA attack on USS *Maddox*
- CHINA
- Gulf of Tonkin
- Vinh
- Ron
- Quang Khe
- LAOS
- Demilitarized Zone (DMZ)
- SOUTH VIETNAM
- CAMBODIA
- US carriers *Constellation* and *Ticonderoga*

* North Vietnamese cities attacked by US airstrikes
* US ship attacked by NVA patrol boats
— US air attacks

Gulf of Tonkin

The 1964 torpedo-boat attack on the *Maddox* was an attempt to drive off US warships supporting secret assaults on North Vietnamese naval bases.

Destroyer insignia

MADDOX
731

USS *Maddox* jacket patch

The Tonkin clash

The *Maddox* was a World War II-era destroyer that had been modernized for electronic surveillance. It was attacked while stationed 4 miles (6 km) off an island base for North Vietnamese patrol boats. The US Navy claimed that these were international waters and that the *Maddox* had a right to be there.

USS *Maddox* officers

Captain John J. Herrick, left, headed a destroyer unit that included the *Maddox*. The commanding officer was Herbert L. Ogier, right. The unit was part of the operation Desoto Patrol.

Shell from Maddox falling into water

Under fire

This photo taken from the *Maddox* shows a North Vietnamese torpedo boat speeding across the horizon. Shells from the warship crash down nearby. Three highspeed boats launched torpedoes at the *Maddox*. The warship's guns damaged all three. Warplanes from the carrier USS *Ticonderoga* joined the fight.

North Vietnamese torpedo boat

McNamara defends war

US secretary of defense Robert S. McNamara explains the *Maddox* clash to reporters. Because of the Gulf of Tonkin Incident, the United States would be "moving substantial military reinforcements" to Southeast Asia.

US F-8 Crusader jet

Air campaign

A warplane roars from the aircraft carrier USS *Constellation* in August 1964. Bombers struck naval bases in the Gulf of Tonkin. In 1965, air attacks expanded into Operation Rolling Thunder, the bombing of supply routes and munitions storage areas. The three-year campaign was stopped several times as LBJ attempted to negotiate with the Communists.

The deck was twice the size of a football field

Medal for heroism

This medal is awarded to Navy personnel for heroism in noncombat situations. Naval duties are often dangerous, especially at sea, and can require great acts of courage.

North Vietnamese torpedo boat

Maddox's cannon fires on torpedo boats

US M-14 rifle

Americanizing the conflict

Although there was no declaration of war, President Johnson used the war powers of the Gulf of Tonkin Resolution to their fullest. He committed the US to Vietnam in a policy known as the Americanization of the war. He hoped US military might would persuade the Communists to accept the South Vietnamese government. In addition to the Rolling Thunder campaign, he sent troops to South Vietnam. The first Marines arrived near Da Nang in March 1965 and soon saw action against the Viet Cong. The Americanization phase of the Second Indochina War— known as the Vietnam War—had begun. By July 1965, more than 50,000 US troops were in South Vietnam.

Marines at the beach

Marines splash ashore near Da Nang, South Vietnam. Additional US forces were arriving elsewhere, and American television showed many of these events. This was the first military conflict to be seen on television.

Allies

Allies were crucial for the Communists. The US and South Vietnam could have waged war alone, but North Vietnam and the Viet Cong needed supplies and financing from China and the Soviet Union. American and RVN forces were aided by Free World Forces: nations in the Southeast Asia Treaty Organization (SEATO). South Korea sent 312,000 troops; Australia sent 47,000. Thailand, the Philippines, and New Zealand also sent soldiers.

Allied propaganda
In this South Vietnamese poster, flags represent the Allied nations. They offer food to the Vietnamese, while the Soviet Union offers only guns.

Chinese munitions
This Chinese-made 120-mm mortar round was captured at a VC supply base in Cambodia.

Soviet money
The USSR gave aid to the Viet Cong. This is a 10-ruble note.

Portrait of Premier Vladimir Ilich Lenin

DRV prime minister Pham Van Dong

A warm welcome in China
North Vietnamese officials receive an enthusiastic greeting from Premier Zhou En-lai on a state visit to Beijing in 1973.

Vietnamese Communist Party leader Le Duan

Chinese premier Zhou En-lai

DRV flag

Clasped hands

Medal
The text reads: "Solidarity against American aggression."

Ho in Russia
Ho Chi Minh joins Soviet officials and leaders from other Communist states at a military parade in Moscow in 1961.

Cuban Communist Party leader Blas Roca

President Ho Chi Minh

Soviet premier Nikita Khrushchev

Hungarian party leader Janos Kadar

Soviet president Leonid Brezhnev

RVN prime minister
Nguyen Cao Ky

Australian
prime minister
Harold Holt

South Korean
president Park
Chung Hee

Philippine president
Ferdinand Marcos

New Zealand
prime minister
Keith Holyoake

RVN chief of state
Nguyen Van Thieu

Thai prime minister
Thanom Kittikachorn

US president
Lyndon B.
Johnson

SEATO leaders in the Philippines

Heads of SEATO nations and nonmembers South Korea and South Vietnam meet in Manila to discuss the Indochina conflict in October 1966. SEATO was founded in 1954 under US direction. Its aim was to prevent more countries in the region from becoming Communist and to support the US in Vietnam. It was disbanded in 1977.

Free World Forces hang tag

This I.D. tag was attached to a button and worn on the shirts of troops that the Allies called Free World Forces (FWF).

Australian service medal

Awards

President Marcos pins medals on Filipino soldiers being honored for bravery in Vietnam in July 1967. He was at headquarters in Tay Ninh, South Vietnam. Filipino troops arrived in Indochina in 1966.

Flower wreath given to welcome President Marcos

Ambush

The 7th Australian Royal Regiment sets up an ambush in hill country. The "Aussies" usually operated guerilla-style. In 1966, a 101-man combat team fought off more than 2,500 VC at Long Tan.

South Korean
White Horse
division patch

US-made
M-1 carbine

South Korean troops

A martial arts instructor shows a flying kick in 1968. Koreans guard VC prisoners, c.1966 (right). South Korea had the third-largest Allied army, after the US and South Vietnam. Koreans maintained three divisions in Vietnam: White Horse, Blue Dragon, and Tiger.

The leaders

At the start of the war, Vietnamese Communist leaders had been in power for more than 20 years and had vast military experience. US and South Vietnamese leaders were mostly politicians. Ho Chi Minh and Vo Nguyen Giap stayed in power for much of the war, while US and RVN leaders came and went. The Communists fought all-out, but the US conducted a "limited war," trying to use only enough force to make the enemy surrender.

"Uncle Ho"
Ho's struggle against French and Japanese occupation prepared him for the Vietnam War. He died before the final Communist triumph in 1975.

Le Duan
Le Duan was a southern Vietminh leader who advanced to first secretary of the Workers Party in 1960. With a reputation for toughness, Le Duan ran the DRV military effort during the war.

Vo Nguyen Giap
General Giap led Communist forces from the 1940s to 1972. Younger generals took over late in the war. Giap retired as minister of defense in 1980.

"We are determined to fight for independence, national unity, democracy, and peace."

HO CHI MINH

Tran Do
Tran Do was deputy commander of Viet Cong forces in South Vietnam. A high-ranking member of the Communist Party, he later fell out with the Communist-led government for criticizing the slow development of Vietnamese democracy.

Pham Van Dong
In 1930, Dong, right, helped Ho found the Indochinese Communist Party. He became prime minister of North Vietnam in 1950.

Nguyen Van Thieu

Shown voting in an election, Thieu was president of South Vietnam from 1967–1973. In the First Indochina War, he fought first for the Vietminh, but then joined the French colonial forces. He later rose to power in South Vietnam. Thieu often tried to control ARVN units in the field, angering his generals.

William C. Westmoreland

General Westmoreland was commander of US forces in Vietnam when the first US combat troops landed in 1965. He was replaced by Creighton Abrams in 1968.

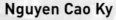

Lyndon B. Johnson campaign button

Lyndon B. Johnson

Johnson feared being the president who let Vietnam become Communist. He is seen, below right, with advisers on *Air Force One*, after meeting South Vietnamese leaders in Hawaii.

Nguyen Cao Ky

A South Vietnamese pilot and air force leader, General Ky was the premier in President Thieu's government from 1965–1971. When Saigon fell in 1975, he fled to America.

"We have no ambition there for ourselves, we seek no wider war."

LYNDON B. JOHNSON

Nixon and Kissinger

President Richard Nixon, left, discusses peace talks with special adviser Henry Kissinger in 1972. Elected in 1968, Nixon chose to prolong the war rather than withdraw and admit defeat.

Saigon and Hanoi

The capital of French Indochina, Hanoi had long been a political, cultural, and economic center. It became the DRV capital in 1954, but Saigon, South Vietnam's capital, soon passed it in wealth and population. Saigon became South Vietnam's military headquarters and boomed from American aid. Hanoi's streets were busy with bicycles; Saigon's roared with cars and scooters. Military vehicles soon appeared in both.

Hanoi politicians
Prime Minister Pham Van Dong, center, attends a government meeting in Hanoi in 1946. Communists dominated the government, but not all North Vietnamese were Communists.

Women home guards
An official registers women in the Hanoi home guard in 1964. The home guard protected the city during conflicts. This often included operating antiaircraft weaponry.

Hanoi

In the colonial period, Hanoi was famous for its restaurants and stylish upper class. After independence, it became a manufacturing hub with top schools and hospitals. Its citizens had suffered under French rule, but they fought on in the war to unify the nation.

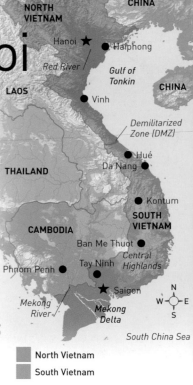

North Vietnam
South Vietnam

Two Vietnams
A major seaport, Saigon was strongly influenced by foreign cultures. Hanoi was influenced by neighboring giant China.

Communist flag

Pushcart

Hanoi in peaceful times
Few North Vietnamese owned motorized vehicles when they prepared for independence in 1954. Bicycles and pushcarts crowded the streets. Hanoi would soon be on its way to becoming a center for government, industry, and higher education.

Saigon

Under the French, Saigon became a modern city with a powerful Vietnamese Roman Catholic elite—most Vietnamese were Buddhist. In 1955, it became the RVN capital and grew rapidly, as 900,000 people fled Communist North Vietnam. US money flowed in, enriching the ruling class. Saigon was notorious for corruption, gambling, prostitution, and the opium trade. By 1965, its population was 1.5 million.

Saigon's old town
The influence of 19th-century French colonial culture is seen in this 1955 street scene. The city's culture, architecture, and nightlife earned it the nickname "Paris of the East."

Heroes returning
Battle-weary ARVN soldiers marching in a Saigon parade in 1961 are given garlands of flowers. The troops had been operating against VC insurgents.

US soldier image

Scrip

Scrip and stolen goods
US forces received "scrip" to buy goods on military bases. In Saigon, it was traded like dollars. Stolen goods from US bases were sold openly.

American goods, smuggled or stolen for the black market

Bustling boulevard
Saigon streets were clogged with scooters and cars in the mid-1960s. Still, the three-wheeled "peditaxi" was a prime means of transportation. Carts powered by cyclists were also essential in the overcrowded city.

Rolling Thunder

The Gulf of Tonkin Incident convinced LBJ's advisers that North Vietnam must be punished. Key adviser McGeorge Bundy believed that bombing the North would prove US resolve. Operation Rolling Thunder began in March 1965. It targeted railroads, airfields, factories, fuel depots, and power plants. Johnson halted bombing seven times, hoping the Communists would ask for peace terms. They did not. He ended the campaign on October 31, 1968.

McGeorge Bundy
Bundy was a security adviser to presidents Kennedy and Johnson. He urged the bombing campaign and helped plan it.

Air force thunderchiefs
Air Force F-105 Thunderchief fighter-bombers are refueled in the air while on their way to bomb North Vietnam in 1966. The refueling aircraft, right, is a KC-135 Stratotanker.

Stratotanker's drogue (refueling device) connects with fighter-bomber to pump in fuel

389th Tactical Fighter Squadron patch

Targets
More than 643,000 tons (574,100 metric tons) of bombs were dropped during Rolling Thunder. US aircraft avoided heavily populated areas around Hanoi and Haiphong, circled. LBJ wanted to minimize civilian casualties.

■ Chinese buffer zone (prohibited to US aircraft)

○ Target restrictions around Hanoi and Haiphong

— US air attacks

CHINA
NORTH VIETNAM
Hanoi
Haiphong
LAOS
Gulf of Tonkin
From Thailand
From S. Vietnam
B-52s from Okinawa
B-52s from Guam
Demilitarized Zone (DMZ)
US 7th Fleet
THAILAND
SOUTH VIETNAM

Successful mission
Navy commander George Jacobssen Jr. signals "okay" after completing a mission against NVA ammunition depots in 1965. American planes were limited to destroying military and economic targets during Rolling Thunder.

A-1 Skyraider warplane

Pilot helmet

Ammunition belt

Bombs fall

F-105 Thunderchiefs following a B-66 Destroyer over North Vietnam release their bombs. The fighter-bombers attacked targets with great accuracy, while high-flying heavy bombers dropped payloads over a wider area. Fighter-bombers flew low to avoid NVA radar.

After a strike

A rail bridge is damaged after a US air strike. Cutting railroads made it hard for the Communists to move equipment and troops. Whenever LBJ halted bombing, the North Vietnamese rebuilt.

Bridge collapsed from precision bombing

Wild Weasel patch

Wild weasel landing

This F-100 fighter's landing is slowed by a tail parachute. The aircraft has radar-jamming equipment that interferes with antiaircraft electronic devices. These "Wild Weasels" specialized in attacking surface-to-air missile (SAM) sites. They flew daringly low as they led other warplanes into action.

Parachute slows plane

Air defense

With Soviet and Chinese aid, Hanoi built a formidable antiaircraft defense. The North Vietnamese Air Force became increasingly effective during Rolling Thunder. Most of its warplanes and antiaircraft weapons were provided by its allies. During Rolling Thunder, the US dropped more bombs on North Vietnam than it had in the Pacific Theater in World War II.

Greeting from VIETNAM

THE VOICE OF VIETNAM
56-58 QUAN SU STREET — HANOI

Home guard

Women in the Hanoi home guard search the skies for US warplanes. Civilians were given weapons and instructed to fire into the air, creating a storm of bullets.

Postcards

Hanoi used propaganda postcards. This card shows a peasant watching a US plane in flames. The pilot was later captured.

Machine gun

Air-raid alarm

A Hanoi resident takes cover in an air-raid shelter. Sirens alerted people to find shelter immediately when US planes were nearby.

Concrete rim

Explosive warhead

Aiming a SAM

A surface-to-air missile crew prepares for an air attack by the US. Thousands of Chinese SAM operators volunteered to serve in North Vietnam. SAMs contained 250 lb (114 kg) of explosives. The US lost 922 aircraft, many shot down by SAMs.

Sheet metal cover

Ho Chi Minh Trail

This wilderness route carried Communist supplies and troops to South Vietnam. From Hanoi, the main trail wound into Laos, while another branch came through Cambodia, often through jungle. There were underground barracks, hospitals, and munitions storage. Supplies moved by foot, bicycle, and even elephant. Much of the 12,500-mile (20,000-km) trail was paved. Late in the war, 3,000 miles (5,000 km) of pipeline carried fuel over mountains and under rivers. By 1970, 20,000 tons (17,850 metric tons) of supplies were moved every month.

Laying steel

NVA engineers fight rushing waters to lay steel girders for a bridge in 1966. Roads and bridges for trucks replaced paths and river fords. Designed by NVA's Logistics Group 559, the project took more than 100,000 workers to build and maintain.

Stairway to war

NVA troops walk down cliff-side steps near the DMZ in 1966. It will take two months for the unit to march to its final position in South Vietnam. The Ho Chi Minh Trail was also called the "Truong Son Road" because it entered the Truong Son Mountains of central Vietnam.

Vast route

Both Laos and Cambodia stayed neutral during the war. Cambodia's Prince Norodom Sihanouk did not want to anger the Communists by blocking the trail, part of which was nicknamed "Sihanouk Trail."

Bicycle warfare

Laborers on the Ho Chi Minh Trail used bicycles to haul ammunition. The bikes had special handles for easier steering. The Communists could not have waged war without the trail to move supplies.

Custom handles

Sulfa drugs

Protecting the health of laborers, soldiers, and the engineering corps was vital for the NVA. The USSR supplied sulfa drugs, which were used to treat bacterial and parasite infections as well as malaria.

Viet Cong sandals

US and ARVN soldiers had modern gear. Communist guerrillas used what they could salvage. These sandals were cut from old rubber tires.

Mountain pass

Communist troops cross misty mountains near the Laos border. As many as 20,000 NVA troops trekked south on the Ho Chi Minh Trail every month. Thousands died from air raids, disease, snake bites, even tigers.

Trail talking

Communication depended on field telephones. This Chinese phone was captured by US troops. Phones at bunkers along the trail were linked by cable.

1.5-volt dry-cell battery for power

Trees killed by US defoliation campaign

Road for trucks

Supply trucks pass through a defoliated part of the trail in the 1970s. Trucks became the heart of the transport system. Engineering battalions had worked by hand at first, but later got Soviet and Chinese roadbuilding equipment.

Chemicals in war

The US wanted to eliminate Viet Cong support in the countryside by destroying food supplies and driving out peasants who aided the VC. The policy of defoliation—killing vegetation with chemical poisons—was enacted. It exposed tree-covered guerrilla bases and supply routes. Agent Orange was sprayed over vast areas. Napalm and white phosphorus (WP) bombs turned lush landscapes into wastelands.

Rostrow
Top adviser Walter W. Rostow urged destroying areas of VC support. Deadly defoliants and napalm were used.

Making napalm
A US soldier mixes chemical thickeners into a gasoline drum to make napalm, a jelly. Upon exploding, flaming globules of napalm stick to everything they touch, causing great suffering.

Destructive payload
Napalm bombs are mounted under the wing of a bomber at Da Nang airfield. Napalm was first used in World War II.

Napalm explosion

Napalm explosions
Liquid fire blossoms into fireballs as a napalm and WP strike blasts a VC hamlet, 1965. The clinging flames of a napalm attack burn for hours on trees and buildings. Napalm was widely used by the US in Vietnam.

Ranch Hand's assault

Operation Ranch Hand was the name of the defoliation campaign operated from 1962 to 1971. The defoliation squadron started with six aircraft, but at its peak in 1969 had 25. It targeted VC bases in Cambodia and South Vietnam. Chemicals were sprayed on jungles and crops by low-flying aircraft. Most jungles could recover from two sprayings, but not three. Mangrove swamps died after one spraying. In all, 19 million gallons (72 million liters) of herbicides were used—60 percent was Agent Orange.

The C-123 aircraft was commonly used in Ranch Hand

Trail of defoliant spray

Patch
Members of the 12th Air Command Squadron wore this patch.

RANCH HAND 紫 VIETNAM

Poisonous spray
Agent Orange can cause illness in humans. US service members and Vietnamese civilians had lasting health problems from contact with the herbicide.

Before and after
The effects of defoliation are seen in this aerial photograph. The field on the right side of the river is brown after being poisoned with Agent Orange. The left bank is still a vibrant green.

Chopper spray
A Huey helicopter sprays defoliant in the Mekong Delta in 1969. The U Minh Forest of mangrove swamps had a dense canopy that hid people and buildings from aircraft. Herbicides killed this, exposing the VC position.

Machine gunner

River through ruin
A man paddles his boat between the bare banks of a former mangrove forest in the Mekong Delta in 1970. Agent Orange destroyed swamps that once were bountiful for fishing.

Sampan propelled by oars

Highlands struggle

In Vietnam's Central Highlands—between Cambodia and the sea—US and Allied forces attacked Viet Cong and NVA strongholds. American bases were under constant threat, and troops operating in the dense forests were frequently ambushed. The Communists' plan was to reach the coast, cut off South Vietnam's northern provinces, and capture them. They lost major battles in the Ia Drang Valley and at Dak To. The Americans found allies in the Montagnard people of the region, who proved especially brave.

Central highlands

Highland valleys could lead Communist forces to the coast. US bases fought to block enemy movements.

NVA forces

NVA troops occupied large areas of the Central Highlands. They were trained in wilderness fighting and could move swiftly and silently. The Americans and ARVN, however, won the major engagements during most of the war.

Nguyen Chi Thanh

General Thanh led a major NVA offensive through the Highlands in 1965. His forces aimed for the sea, but were stopped at Ia Drang Valley.

Ammo pouch

This ammunition belt is typical NVA "webbing," the term for military belts and pouches made of fabric.

Communist star

NVA helmet

NVA soldiers wore light but sturdy helmets that protected them from sun and rain.

Strap

Tube scarf

NVA soldiers carried their daily ration of rice in a tubelike scarf that kept it secure.

Double spout

NVA oil can

This can held oil used to maintain weaponry.

Fastening loop

Ammunition clip

NVA canteen

Communist fighters carried little gear compared to US and ARVN troops. They had to travel fast and live off the land. A water canteen was vital.

Harness strap

Elite forces and allies

US "Green Beret" Special Forces were active in the Central Highlands. Operating in small teams, they used guerrilla tactics and made loyal allies of the local Montagnard people, whom Green Beret units equipped and trained. French for "mountain-dwellers," the Montagnard were fiercely independent. They first opposed the South Vietnamese government, but the Special Forces made an alliance. Other elite US forces in the area included troopers of the Air Cavalry and Airborne. When the NVA attacked at Dak To in 1967, the troopers defeated them.

Chopper landing
A Green Beret waves in a supply helicopter. The US Special Forces' isolated mountain bases were supplied by air, but the men often lived off the land. They faced danger daily.

Green beret

Setting up a highland base
A Chinook transport helicopter supplies US Airmobile troopers at a new mountaintop base in 1967. The Americans are on a search-and-destroy operation. The landing zone is codenamed LZ Quick, which the NVA tries to ambush.

Land navigation
This soldier wears a position locator to find his way. It has a pedometer step sensor that determines his stride length. The device tells the soldier where he is in relation to where he started.

AIRBORNE

Green Beret Airborne patch

Pedometer step sensor

M-60 machine gun

Air Cavalry patch
Insignia bears the title of the regiment's song: "Garry Owen."

Taking aim
This 101st Airborne trooper is under fire in the battle of Dak To. Fierce fighting lasted three weeks. Victory came on Thanksgiving Day.

Crossbow bolts

Quiver

Wooden body

Montagnard men
Montagnard soldiers armed with US submachine guns prepare for patrol. Special Forces teams began training Montagnards as early as 1963, during the advisory period of the Vietnam War.

Crossbow
This traditional weapon of the mountain people could be deadly in counter-guerrilla warfare. It fired short arrows called crossbow bolts.

Weaponry

The war was waged with both sophisticated and primitive weapons. US firearms were matched by Soviet and Chinese weaponry. The VC also used booby traps. The support of villagers was essential to VC resistance in the South. Women set booby traps, and men made mines from spent shell casings. The war was decided by ground action that required fierce courage on both sides.

Claymore
The US Claymore antipersonnel mine fired 700 steel balls 100 yards (90 m) in a 60-degree arc.

Nva gun
NVA troops used this 75-mm recoilless rifle.

NVA and VC forces

The Soviets and China provided North Vietnam with huge quantities of arms. Well-armed NVA troops controlled parts of South Vietnam and operated in fairly large units. The VC, however, moved in small units in the shadow of US and ARVN forces. VC often used weapons captured from their enemies. The Claymore antipersonnel mine was one of the deadliest.

Bomb-making
VC soldiers salvage US shell casings and unexploded artillery ammo. They reload the casings to make explosive devices. Grenades were put in booby traps.

Grenades

Soviet-made AK-47
Rapid-firing AK-47 assault rifles were the most important firearms carried by Communist troops.

Ammunition magazine

NVA knife

Communist star

Grenade launcher
The rocket-propelled grenade launcher (RPG) fires warheads that can penetrate armor, destroying armored trucks and tanks.

Rocket exhaust vent

Telescopic sight

Warhead holds explosive

Rocket-propelled grenade

Sharpened bamboo

Stakes
Villagers sharpened bamboo into punji stakes for booby traps. The stakes were set in pits and covered by branches and leaves, which give way when stepped on.

Trigger and magazine

SKS Simonov carbine
The bayonet of an SKS rifle folded into a support when the soldier fired lying down.

Free World Forces

The Free World Forces used weapons similar to the Communists: assault rifles and grenade launchers. Although far better than the weaponry of the VC, FWF weapons were matched by NVA arms. The FWF had the advantage of artillery and a supply line. The Communists had almost no artillery and depended on weapons supplied via the Ho Chi Minh Trail. FWF troops were resupplied by planes and helicopters.

M-1 bayonet

Flash hider

Launcher attached to end of barrel

Grenade and adaptor for M-1 carbine

Grenade

M1
ARVN troops were often equipped with older US firearms, such as this M-1 carbine. The M-1 had a bayonet and fired rifle grenades and bullets.

30-round magazine

Barrel of grenade launcher

Sight for grenade launcher

M-16 cleaning kit
Firearms must be cleaned and oiled to work. This US M-16 kit is used to swab the barrel.

Handle for cleaning rod

Cleaning fluid

Cleaning brush attaches to rod

Hinge to fold rod compactly into a pouch

Cleaning brush

M-16 bayonet

Bayonet sheath

US assault rifle
The M-16A1 offers more than the M-16 assault rifle's burst of automatic fire and 30-round magazine. It has a grenade launcher fixed under the muzzle.

US grenades
The infantry carried grenades. The ring for the pin was pulled, and after the soldier threw the grenade, a fuse would light. In a few seconds, the grenade exploded.

Sight

Front sling fitting

"Blooper"
The US M-79 grenade launcher, nicknamed Blooper, has a range of 50–300 yards (46–274 m) and sends 300 metal fragments over a wide area.

Rear sling fitting

Ring is pulled before throwing

Pineapple grenade

Baseball grenade

Lemon grenade

M-60 machine gun
A Special Forces soldier fires an M-60 7.62-mm machine gun at enemy positions. The belt-fed gun was one of the most important weapons available to American forces in the war. It was used by small-unit operations and was mounted on choppers.

155-MM Howitzer
ARVN artillerymen used the 155-mm howitzer. Shells take a high trajectory, so defenses that resist direct fire are vulnerable to shells dropping from above.

On patrol

The fighting in Vietnam required foot soldiers. Soldiers patrolled villages to protect locals from the VC or NVA, who often lay in wait. Reconnaissance missions—by platoons or companies of 20 to 100 men—were done to learn about enemy units. The aim of search-and-destroy missions was to kill or capture the enemy. In a firefight, the commander radioed for air or artillery support.

Bearings
An infantryman on patrol in unfamiliar territory uses a compass to determine his location. The Lensatic military compass has a front sight and a magnifying lens and folds into a carrying case.

Sighting wire, with rear-sight slot and lens to sight on objects

Rear-sight slot

Lens enlarges dial

Insect repellent

Jungle boots
Waterproof boots were essential.

Waterproof material

Infantry helmet
The helmet strap could hold Army-issue cigarettes and bug repellent.

Grenade

Collapsible shovel

Food pouch

Canteen

Ammo pouch

M18 SMOKE VIOLET

1701-9054

Ammo pouch

Smoke grenade

Bayonet in scabbard

Day-pack gear
Fully loaded, this gear belt for day patrol is 60 lb (27 kg). It holds ammo, a shovel, bayonet, canteen, first-aid kit, and food.

Handset (phone)

Short-range antenna

Radio controls

Collecting water
A 1st Infantry Division soldier on patrol refills his canteen. Halazone, a bacteria-killing powder, was added to make the water safe to drink.

AN/PRC-25 backpack field radio

Calling the base
A radioman carries a field radio as his commanding officer talks to the base. Patrols set out from fire bases—encampments with headquarters, artillery, and troops. A patrol could radio for enemy positions to be shelled or call for help.

Five-quart inflatable canteen

Vial of halazone water purifier

Instructions for inflating canteen

VC ambush

The Viet Cong were skilled at ambush. They hid in trees, fields, and even underground. They often struck in a hail of gunfire and grenades. The lead patrol—the man "on point"—was in particular danger. If outnumbered, the VC melted back into the countryside. If superior in force, they would try to wipe out the patrol before air support arrived.

In the open
Troops of the 9th Infantry Division turn toward possible enemy movement as they walk across a rice paddy. Patrols were exposed to attack, especially as they entered forests, villages, or open fields. This is a day patrol, since the soldiers carry little gear. Long-range reconnaissance patrols went into the field for days.

Watching and waiting
A VC fighter lies in a ditch, his rifle ready. He is part of a force waiting to ambush a US or ARVN patrol.

Demonstrating tactics
Posing for the camera, VC guerrillas show how to hide in haystacks. In combat, they would disappear under the hay if an enemy patrol approached. If the patrol was too strong, they let it pass. If not, they attacked.

Medical care

In 1965, the US had two 100-bed military hospitals in Vietnam. By 1969, 30 hospitals, with 5,000 beds, and two hospital ships were staffed by 16,000 doctors, 15,000 nurses, and thousands of support staff. On the battlefield, medics bandaged the wounded. Emergency flights took the injured to hospitals. Communist medical care was primitive. Their wounded were carried to field hospitals hidden in swamps, caves, or tunnels.

Medevac
"Dustoff" on this pilot's belt buckle is a nickname for ambulance helicopters.

Extra bandages

Medic's kit
A medic's kit included bandages, gauze, tape, antiseptics, and medical status cards to identify the patient and document injury.

U.S. FIELD MEDICAL CARD

Medical status cards

Wires to attach cards to patients

Wire splint for broken arm or leg

First-aid tape *Gauze bandages* *Sterilized first-aid dressing*

Evacuating a wounded soldier
An injured Marine is helped to safety as a medic holds a blood transfusion kit. Advances in medical care resulted in fewer than one in five US wounded dying from injuries. In World War II, one in three died of their wounds.

Medevac chopper arrives
A medevac (medical evacuation) helicopter picks up wounded troops in 1966. The pilot homes in on the purple smoke-cloud that signals where to land. After loading the wounded and taking off, choppers were often targets of gunfire. Many soldiers were treated within 20 minutes of being injured.

M18 SMOKE VIOLET

1701-9054

Purple smoke grenade

Rigid litter basket

Basket
A helicopter lowers a rigid litter basket to be loaded with an injured soldier. Often, helicopters could not land in dense jungle. Litters were lowered by cable, and the wounded were hauled up from the battlefield.

Saving a life

A surgical team performs an emergency operation at a US field hospital in 1969. Male doctors were usually drafted into the military, but women were volunteers. Seriously injured patients were flown to military hospitals in Japan or Okinawa for further treatment.

First stop

The chopper's red cross symbolizes a medical unit, which was not to be fired upon. Medevac helicopters were shot regardless, and some were lost.

President George Washington

Dog tags

All troops wear "dog tags" around their necks. The metal tags are stamped with the soldier's personal data.

Injured in combat

More than 200,700 Purple Heart medals were awarded during the Indochina conflict.

Blood pressure cuff

Mosquito netting

Communist med units

Communist field hospitals in South Vietnam were camouflaged to prevent bombing attacks by American and ARVN forces. Their sparse medical supplies came mostly from China or the USSR. Serving long periods in the jungle, VC and NVA fighters suffered greatly from tropical diseases and fever.

Chinese penicillin bottle

晶青霉素钾
PENICILLIN
500000单位
批号: 09024 有效期
国营华北製药

Wooden pole for carrying hammock with patient

Journey for aid

Communist soldiers carry a wounded comrade on a hammock litter suspended on a bamboo pole. They trek through difficult terrain to the nearest medical facility.

Wood-and-canvas stretcher

Operating in a swamp

Viet Cong nurses and doctors work knee-deep in water in a field hospital. The stretcher-bearer waits to bring a patient to the operating table.

Heliborne warfare

Helicopters came into wide use in Vietnam. Until then, they had been used for scouting and airlifting wounded. In the 1960s, US "choppers" were improved in power and armaments. They rushed soldiers into action, fired on the enemy, and moved supplies. The NVA had no helicopters.

Harry Kinnard
General Kinnard led the 1st Cavalry Division, the first unit to be transported by helicopter. Called airmobile or heliborne troops, they went to Vietnam in 1965.

M-16 rifle

Air cavalry
Troopers of the 1st Air Cavalry Division hit the ground running as they jump from a Huey during a scouting mission. "Air Cav" troops were the world's first heliborne soldiers. Their success led to the widespread use of helicopters and airmobile units.

Landing skids

Supply pouch

Rocket on target
Covering fire from the air supported ground troops, who communicated by radio during combat. This type of chopper was nicknamed Huey, for its model name: UH-1.

Gunners
A machine gunner looks for VC from the air. Gunners were favorite enemy targets. Their duty was one of the most dangerous.

Huey weaponry
The Huey's armaments included seven-pod aerial-rocket launchers and rapid-firing machine guns, such as the "minigun" (left).

Rockets

Helicopter wing

Machine gun ammunition belt

Pilot and copilot positions

Helicopter landing wheel

Heavy machine gun

Fuselage and tail

Cobra attack helicopter
The AH-1W Sea Cobra was one of the first attack helicopters, introduced in 1967. These "gunships" escorted fast transport helicopters. The heavily armed Huey was a workhorse, but was too slow to keep up with transport choppers. Used by the Marines and Army, Cobras were swift and agile, with great firepower.

Pilot and copilot positions

Cannon

Insignia

Pilots and mechanics wore special patches. These units of the 7th Squadron, 1st Cavalry Regiment, called themselves "Apache Aeroscouts" and "King Birds."

Apache Aeroscouts

King Birds

Cargo helicopters

The Americans and ARVN operated thousands of helicopters during the war, with four main models: utility for general use; observation for scouting; attack gunships for battle; and cargo for transporting supplies around the country. Models were always being updated.

U.S. ARMY 03450

ARMY

Chinook

The mighty CH-47 Chinook was one of the best cargo aircraft of the war. These heavy-lifting helicopters frequently transported field guns. Here, a gun is suspended beneath the body of a US Army Chinook, in flight to a distant base.

Landing wheel

Cannon barrel

Cannon limber

Field cannon

Flying crane

Rotors

This CH-54A Skycrane transport helicopter was dubbed a "Flying Crane" for its ability to lift heavy loads. The Skycrane often moved guns and vehicles into isolated bases, where soldiers built artillery positions to prepare for battle.

Tail-mounted rotor

Cutaway design for large cargo

Tall landing gear for cutaway

Warplanes

Rolling Thunder struck North Vietnamese roads, railroads, and bridges to slow the supply chain. Bombing population centers was not permitted because LBJ did not want civilian casualties. The US F-105 fighter-bombers were targets for antiaircraft fire. By the end of 1966, 455 US warplanes had been shot down. In January 1967, superior US fighters won a dramatic victory over the North's Soviet-made MiG-21s. By the end of 1967, the bombing campaign had devastated North Vietnam, but the US had lost 649 aircraft.

Fighter pilot
The glow of the instrument panel lights the face of a US F-4 fighter pilot. He is preparing for a night mission from Da Nang air base.

F-4D Phantom cockpit

Flight helmet

Stars symbolize a kill

Top US ace
Captain Charles DeBellevue flew 220 combat missions and shot down six MiGs.

Tricking NVAF defenders

The NVAF's MiG-21s took on the slower F-105s but avoided the F-4 Phantoms. On January 2, 1967, Colonel Robin Olds led his 8th Tactical Fighter Wing in Operation Bolo, aiming to draw MiGs into action. His F-4s flew in formation with F-105s and used F-105 radio call-signs. MiG-21s were surprised by the F-4s. Seven MiG-21s were shot down, with no US losses.

US Air Force symbol on aircraft

Fuselage

Rear horizontal wing stabilizes plane

Air-to-air missile

Colonel's eagle

Harness for parachute

Bolo leader
Colonel Robin Olds shot down one of the seven MiG-21s during Operation Bolo. He eventually shot down four enemy aircraft and earned the Air Force Cross for extraordinary heroism.

MiG-killers
F-4 Phantoms fly in formation in 1967. This formidable fighter escorted older and less maneuverable F-105 fighter-bombers in missions over the North. The F-4 was the best fighter of the day, flying at 1,600 mph (2,500 kph). They were termed "MiG killers."

Vest with pouches

Inflation hose controls air pressure in flight suit

Flight suit

Air Force Cross

Bald eagle symbolizes the United States and air striking power.

Dogfight

Viewed through the 20-mm cannon sight of a pursuing F-105, a MiG is hit on the wing. The older F-105 fighter-bombers were often at a disadvantage to NVAF MiGs in aircraft-to-aircraft engagements known as dogfights. This F-105 next passed 20 feet (7 m) beneath the doomed MiG.

NVAF ace

Pham Thanh Ngan, the fourth-leading NVAF ace, wears a medal for each of his eight kills. NVAF pilots were trained by China and the USSR and flew aircraft made by those countries.

Ho Chi Minh

Air Medal

Medal

Pilots got this for downing Allied planes.

Preparing for takeoff

In the cockpit of his MiG-21, third-best NVAF ace, Mai Van Cuong, readies for a mission. Cuong recorded eight kills. The top ace, Nguyen Van Coc, had nine. MiG-21s were flown by 12 of the 16 aces. A pilot becomes an ace after five kills. The NVAF's 16 aces accounted for 106 of the 169 US warplanes shot down in air-to-air combat.

MiG cockpit

Cockpit cover

Second cockpit for weapons system officer

20-mm cannon sight

Pilot's cockpit

Engine exhaust

Air base

A crew services a fighter at an NVAF airfield outside Hanoi. US bombers avoided population centers, so NVAF aircraft were based near the city.

M-61A1 20-mm cannon

Nose

Serial number

NVAF symbol on aircraft

Soviet MiG-21

The MiG-21 was designed as a fast interceptor to drive off attacking enemy aircraft. This highly agile fighter flew at 1,385 mph (2,200 kph) and was armed with air-to-air missiles. It was a short-range fighter. Between 1965 and 1973, US warplanes downed 68 MiG-21s. Few NVAF fighter pilots survived the war.

Landing gear

The Television War

The Vietnam War was called the first "Television War," because TV brought the horrors of war into homes as never before. At first, the media supported the war, reporting on the military situation, but not explaining Vietnam's struggle against foreign rule. As the conflict worsened, the government pretended it was going well. Some journalists, such as Walter Cronkite, began to call for peace.

At the typewriter
Neil Sheehan reported about the Vietnam War for United Press International (UPI) and *The New York Times*. He later exposed government lies about the war.

Bronze Star

Fighting reporter
UPI's Joseph Galloway often fought alongside the troops he covered. He won a Bronze Star for rescuing a wounded man.

News film camera

Microphone

Sound monitor

Interviewing soldiers
Reporters from CBS news interview US soldiers about a recent battle in 1967. Military commanders gave journalists considerable freedom to meet the troops.

Helmet with AP logo

Aiming with a camera
Vietnamese photographer Huynh Thanh My lies in muddy water under enemy fire while on assignment for the Associated Press (AP). My covered ARVN troops fighting in the Mekong Delta in 1965. He was killed later that year.

Young photojournalist
Twelve-year-old Lo Manh Hung checks his camera while taking pictures in Saigon in 1968. At 10, this Vietnamese youth began working with his father, a photojournalist. Hung wears a military helmet labeled "Press" in English and Vietnamese.

Helping the injured
In 1975, UPI photographer Willy Vicoy carries a wounded girl to safety after rockets hit near Cambodia's capital, Phnom Penh. Press members often put off covering events to take part in them, usually to help the injured.

Stars and Stripes *patch*

News about his war

A 9th Division soldier reads the Army's daily newspaper, *Stars and Stripes*, which tells of military action and antiwar protests. The paper was respected for its accurate reporting.

Press pass

War correspondents had press cards. Frances FitzGerald's reporting won her fame.

Department of Defense seal

NVA news

VC general Tran Van Tra is at a press conference. Like the US and South Vietnam, Communist officials limited information about the war. Newspapers were the main North Vietnamese source of news. The nation's first TV network went into service in 1970.

Pentagon conference

US secretary of defense Robert McNamara, at the Pentagon in 1967, answers journalists' questions. The government's daily press conferences often gave reporters overly optimistic or misleading reports.

Map of Vietnam

Walter Cronkite and Vietnam

CBS anchor Cronkite dismayed many Americans by comparing the destruction and loss in Vietnam to World War II, which he had covered, and criticizing US policy. LBJ said, "If I've lost Cronkite, I've lost middle America."

Exposing the truth

In 1971, former Pentagon staffer Daniel Ellsberg gave *The New York Times* secret documents detailing government lies about the war. Neil Sheehan reported on these in "The Pentagon Papers." By now, most wanted the war to end.

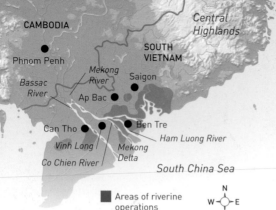

CAMBODIA

Phnom Penh

Bassac
River

*Mekong
River*

Ap Bac

**SOUTH
VIETNAM**

*Central
Highlands*

Saigon

Can Tho

Ben Tre

Ham Luong River

Vinh Long

Co Chien River

*Mekong
Delta*

South China Sea

■ Areas of riverine
operations

N
W—◇—E
S

Mekong Delta

The 2,800-mile (4,500-km) Mekong River
deposits fine soil as it empties into the
South China Sea, building up a delta (sandy
lowland). Near the Mekong Delta is Saigon,
South Vietnam's largest city. The areas
shaded in blue on the map show US and
ARVN riverine operations against the VC.

The Mekong Delta

The Mekong Delta, covered in waterlogged rice
paddies, is Indochina's "rice bowl." At the mouth
of the Mekong River, it is 26,000 square miles
(67,340 sq km). The delta was a guerrilla
stronghold in the Indochina wars. US and ARVN
forces established bases there. Gunboats
looking to destroy VC positions passed along
the waterways. Infantry patrolled on foot.
Aircraft struck guerrilla positions. The
VC held on, aided by local villagers.

Strike mission

Flames and smoke rise from a
rocket attack by an American
UH-1A Iroquois helicopter in the
Mekong Delta. Twisting waterways
and patchwork rice paddies are
surrounded by dense woods that
shelter VC guerrillas.

*Flames from
rocket strike*

Under the gun

An ARVN personnel carrier's
machine gun aims at the
Mekong Delta horizon as a
farmer plows his rice paddy.
The government often
destroyed crops to keep
them from the VC, which
angered farmers. Some
began siding with the VC.

*Swamp buffalo serve as draft
animals for rice cultivation*

Viet Cong fighter

Guerrilla sentry Soc Trang stands at
her post in the Mekong Delta, in 1973.
Trang was just 24, but had already been
widowed twice. Both husbands were VC
soldiers who died in action. The VC and
North Vietnamese forces counted many
women among their fighters in the field.
Trang carries a captured US M-16 rifle.

Mekong hamlet

This view from an aircraft in 1968 shows a remote hamlet in the Mekong River. The river is just a few feet deep near the houses. Boats are the main transportation, but houses are linked by raised paths that have been used for centuries.

Path between houses

Thatched roof

Poling homeward

A Mekong Delta family uses poles to push a boat through the waters surrounding their hamlet. A neighbor building a new house works on the roof's ridge pole. The typical home is framed with poles and covered with a thatched roof—a blanket of dried leaves or straw held down by rope and poles. The houses stand on earthen bases above the water level.

Captured US M-16 rifle

Poles support racks for drying fishing nets

US soldier's patch

The 9th Infantry Division served in the Mekong. It was a difficult service, with frequent VC ambushes and a brutal climate.

Monitor in the Mekong

An armed and armored Monitor gunboat churns past a village in the Mekong Delta in an operation against the VC. The Navy gunboat is headed to a nearby base, where other military craft are gathered. The crew of a US vessel docked ahead watches the gunboat.

War on inland waters

In 1965, the US Navy began patrolling South Vietnam's 3,000 miles (4,800 km) of inland waterways. In the swampy Mekong and Saigon river deltas, Communist forces dominated villages and farms. To penetrate these strongholds, in 1967, MACV established the Mobile Riverine Force. It combined Army troops with crews of Navy patrol boats, armored gunboats, and napalm-firing boats. Large vessels served as floating barracks. Riverine units, which operated in muddy water, were called the "Brown Water Navy." They struck deep into enemy territory.

Elmo R. Zumwalt
Called the "Father of the Brown Water Navy," Admiral Zumwalt led US naval forces in Vietnam from 1968 to 1970.

Naval patches
Each Navy unit had its own patch. Sailors of the USS *White River*, a World War II ship, wore a design with an eagle atop a cannon. The River Patrol Force patch had lightning and swords. The River Assault Division 91 patch showed a "River Rat."

River Assault Division 91 patch

Patch of the River Patrol Force, Task Force 116

USS *White River* naval patch

Gunboat
A Monitor patrols the Mekong Delta in 1967. These armored vessels were named after Union gunboats of the Civil War.

50-mm cannon

Rotating armored gun turret

Reinforced steel hull

Frame for canvas roof

Loading ramp falls forward onto river bank when landing troops

Patrolling the Mekong
A Navy task force travels through the VC-held Mekong Delta in 1967. Armored assault boats were part of the Riverine Force. They took part in Operation Coronado and inflicted heavy losses on the enemy.

Thick steel armor protects troops

Pole used to propel craft and for steering

ARVN ride a sampan
South Vietnamese troops, in the southern province of Ca Mau, return to camp in a native craft loaded with firewood. South Vietnam had a modern navy, but its riverine forces often used the traditional sampan.

A Navy Zippo blast

Deadly flame boats were nicknamed "Zippos," after a popular brand of cigarette lighter. Guns on the turrets shot streams of flaming napalm up to 200 yards (180 m), destroying everything in range. Napalm jelly sticks to its target and keeps burning. In ambushes, the VC often attacked the dangerous Zippos first.

Burning out VC

Primitive, but effective, the flaming arrow being fired from this US officer's bow will set the straw roofs of a Viet Cong riverbank base on fire. Such strikes avoided the need to land troops.

Radar mast   *Pilothouse*

Deckhouse

Swift boat on patrol

A Navy Swift boat makes a highspeed run in South Vietnam's Cam Ranh Bay. The Swifts, officially termed "patrol craft fast" (PCF), served along the coast and on inland rivers. Each speedy Swift was equipped with a machine gun and an 81-mm mortar.

Shark mouth

Fiercely decorated, fast-moving patrol air-cushion vehicles (PACVs) were able to cross swamps and rice paddies. Hovercraft transported troops for surprise missions and could move quickly to block enemy escape routes.

Shark-tooth bow design

Village life

Vietnamese peasants lived much as their ancestors had, planting, harvesting, and fishing. VC fighters depended on villagers and threatened those who did not cooperate. US and ARVN troops ordered locals not to aid the VC. Peasants tried to keep farming, but soldiers on both sides often punished them for helping the opposition. In 1968, US troops massacred My Lai villagers, turning more Americans against the war.

Rings of bamboo walls

Sharpened bamboo

Strategic hamlets
In the early 1960s, South Vietnam built fortified towns guarded by militia. These "strategic hamlets" were surrounded by fences and ditches. Peasants were moved in to keep them from the VC. The program ended after a few years.

Coming close
A helicopter drops low to investigate villagers tending buffalo. ARVN troops are in the background. Peasants never knew whether soldiers would think they were VC and fire on them. Life in a combat zone was dangerous.

After action
ARVN soldiers talk with peasants after an engagement with VC guerrillas. The soldiers had just fought off a VC ambush, and an ARVN lieutenant was killed. His body lies in the bottom of the boat. If the soldiers think villagers helped the VC, their huts will likely be burned.

On trial
A "people's court" led by the VC tries a youth accused of aiding the ARVN. He was found guilty and sentenced to two years in prison. A companion was sentenced to death.

Pacification program

A US chaplain demonstrates a toy trumpet to Vietnamese children. Bringing food and humanitarian aid was part of a relief program known as the Pacification Program. The aim was to "win the hearts and minds" of people.

Dwellings

Shoulder basket

Searching for Communists

Air Cavalry troopers search a house for NVA or VC soldiers. The troopers are in the Highlands, where NVA troops operated. Their mission is to clear out Communists, whose agents could be among the civilians.

Chores in a war zone

Peasant women carrying shoulder baskets meet US Marines assembling on a road. The women keep to the middle as the troops part to let them pass.

Massacre at My Lai

Army Americal Division soldiers entered My Lai village on March 16, 1968, with orders to find the enemy. The troops believed the villagers were VC sympathizers. Under the command of Lt. William L. Calley Jr., they shot more than 300 men, women, and children. Others were saved when a US helicopter crew threatened to fire on Calley's men. The military tried to cover up the massacre. Some soldiers were indicted for murder; only Calley was convicted.

Fire and death

After killing civilians, the soldiers burned My Lai. There were no reports of troops being attacked. A year later, a former soldier wrote to President Nixon, the Pentagon, and members of Congress about the atrocity, which became public. Many Americans were outraged, and the antiwar movement gained strength.

Calley to court

William Calley, center, and his military and civilian attorneys arrive for a pretrial hearing in Fort Benning, Georgia, in January 1970. Many Americans believed Calley should not have been punished because both sides had killed civilians. Calley was sentenced to life imprisonment, but President Nixon had the sentence reduced to 20 years. Later, Nixon granted Calley parole after the officer had spent just three days in a military jail.

Tunnels

The Vietnamese dug tunnels in the First Indochina War and continued to do so in the Vietnam War in Communist-controlled areas of South Vietnam. Guerrillas lived in the tunnels, which had bedrooms, kitchens, munitions depots, and hospitals. When US or Allied troops passed by, fighters hid in the tunnels or made surprise attacks. Brave Allied volunteers went into the tunnels.

Viet Cong tunnels

Vietnamese laborers use crude tools to dig a tunnel entrance. They lift out dirt-filled baskets, empty them, then send them back in. When complete, this part of the tunnel will be covered, hidden from view.

Wooden plug

Shrapnel pieces

VC antipersonnel mine

Trigger mechanism

Booby traps

The VC set traps to injure enemy troops coming into tunnel systems. Traps included mines detonated by trip wires and even poisonous snakes, such as vipers or cobras.

Chinese cobra

SKS Simonov carbine

Cu Chi

The largest complex—with 155 miles (250 km) of tunnels—was at Cu Chi, 45 miles (75 km) north of Saigon. This illustration is from the Cu Chi Museum. Complexes had electricity, underwater entrances, air shafts, and headquarters.

Hidden entrance

Underwater entry

Guard post

Air shafts

Sentry post

ĐỊA ĐẠO CỦ CHI
TRONG BÁO CÁO CỦA OÉT-MO-LEN
GỞI TỔNG THỐNG MỸ

Meeting room

Airtight platform protects against flooding

Rice cooker

Wood stoves

On guard

A VC sentry waiting underground is alert for possible enemy discovery of his tunnel. The entrance to the tunnel is on the right.

Cover keeps out bugs and rodents

Underground kitchen

Tunnel kitchens had vents that sent smoke in many directions so it wasn't seen above ground. Some VC lived underground for months. They emerged for quick attacks and just as suddenly vanished into the tunnels.

Wash bucket

Returning tunnel rat

A US soldier is pulled from a tunnel he searched. Americans were generally larger than Vietnamese and had trouble with the narrow tunnels. This man wears a gas mask against the tear gas he threw into the tunnel.

Flak jacket

Gas mask

Flashlight

Tunnel rats

"Tunnel rats" were a special breed of soldier who took on one of the most dangerous, frightening duties of the war. They risked their lives by crawling into VC tunnels to see if a tunnel led to a major complex. Armed with a pistol, a knife, and a flashlight, the soldier squirmed through twisting, dark tunnels, where he might find a sentry, a booby trap—or nothing at all.

Gas and gas mask

Pull-ring

Before entering a tunnel, a tunnel rat would toss in a tear-gas canister to force away guards. Wearing a gas mask, he then crawled inside.

Handle

GAS CN-DM

PB-2-68

Tear gas

Air filter

Tear gas mask

Strap

Special non-rolling design

Belt clip

Tunnel gear

The .45 pistol was the tunnel rat's most potent weapon, but he also carried a "Ka-Bar" combat knife. Sometimes soldiers encountered enemies in the tunnels, and deadly shootouts resulted.

.45 caliber bullet

.45 pistol

Bullet and magazine

Flashlight

Tight fit

A 173rd Airborne Division engineer squats in a tunnel in the "Iron Triangle," a VC stronghold north of Saigon. His unit is searching for VC caches of ammo.

Hilt

Handle

Ka-Bar knife

Ka-Bar sheath

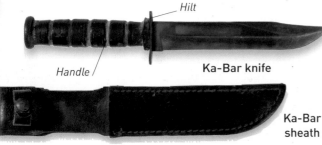
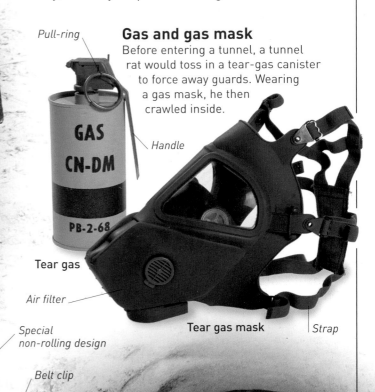

Tet Offensive

On January 21, 1968, the Communists ambushed a Marine base at Khe Sanh. Hanoi's offensive then erupted in South Vietnam on January 30, during the Vietnamese New Year, known as "Tet." In four weeks, the Tet Offensive struck 100 cities and towns. The Communists lost, but the US knew the war would drag on.

The monkey
The Vietnamese give each year a Chinese zodiac animal symbol: 1968 was the Year of the Monkey, a creature thought to be vengeful.

Map labels: NORTH VIETNAM, Demilitarized Zone (DMZ), THAILAND, Khe Sanh, Quang Tri, Hué, Phu Bai, Da Nang, LAOS, Pleiku, CAMBODIA, SOUTH VIETNAM, Mekong River, Ban Me Thuot, Central Highlands, Phnom Penh, Tay Ninh, Bien Hoa, Duc Hoa, Saigon, Phan Thiet, Moc Hoa, Vinh Long, Mekong Delta, South China Sea, Ca Mau

Battle sites
Areas of fighting
Ho Chi Minh Trail

Khe Sanh

Khe Sanh's 6,000 Marines and ARVN troops blocked enemy supply routes from Laos. The Communist siege of early 1968 drew Allied forces from the cities, which were soon attacked. Thousands of US and Allied troops battled to reach the base, which held out for 77 days before relief arrived.

Tet offensive
Bases and government buildings in South Vietnam faced fierce assaults, particularly in Hué and Saigon.

The president studies Khe Sanh
LBJ and advisers examine a model of besieged Khe Sanh. He believed Giap wanted to turn Khe Sanh into another Dien Bien Phu, forcing the US to withdraw, as the French had in 1954. The US anxiously followed the course of the siege.

US M-101 howitzer

Khe Sanh artillery
US gunners return enemy artillery fire. Marines and South Vietnamese allies fought to drive off infantry attacks. Every week, they were hit with 2,500 rounds of artillery, mortars, and rockets.

Explosion at Khe Sanh
Marines duck as a munitions storage pit takes a direct hit. Like Dien Bien Phu, Khe Sanh was surrounded by hills with Communist gun positions. The Americans, however, had overwhelming air power. Helicopters braved hostile fire, bringing in supplies and evacuating wounded. Relief forces fought their way through on April 8, ending the siege.

Saigon

The main struggle of the Tet Offensive was the battle for Saigon. Nineteen VC guerrillas broke into the US embassy and fought for hours before being wiped out. In an assault on MACV headquarters at Tan Son Nhut airfield, US and Allied forces, led by General Weyand, fought off every VC attack, defeating them by February 5.

Frederick C. Weyand
As commander of II Field Force (which defended Saigon), General Weyand was warned of a coming assault and pulled his forces nearer to Saigon. His success during Tet earned him promotion to overall command in Vietnam.

South Vietnamese flag

Hué

The battle for Hué ended March 2. Part of this ancient city was imperial Vietnam's capital. Fighting destroyed much of Hué and its Imperial Citadel. The Communists lost Tet, but they won political victory: more Americans now opposed the war. Tet was the turning point of the war, which increasingly favored the Communists.

Saigon recovers
Saigon had seen little violence before Tet. Afterward, residents had to pick their way through rubble to search for victims and clean up their homes.

Viet Cong in Hué
As the battle rages, a VC soldier radios Communist troops in Hué. He is in the Imperial Citadel.

VIETNAMESE RANGER 35 BN

ARVN Ranger patch

ARVN retakes Citadel
Weary South Vietnamese troops planted their flag on Hué's shattered Citadel. US and ARVN forces attacked VC and NVA fighters at the fortress, while Allied warplanes blasted enemy-occupied buildings.

After the battle
Members of the US Fifth Marine Regiment patrol a war-torn street in Hué. These troops reinforced Allied units and fought for three brutal weeks to recapture the city. The destroyed Imperial Citadel is in the background.

Antiwar movement

Peace signs
The peace symbol, top, protested nuclear weapons. In 1968, the *V* for victory became a sign for antiwar Democrats.

By 1965, many Americans opposed the war. That year, more than 20,000 demonstrators marched in Washington, D.C. At first, supporters and opponents joined in peaceful "teach-ins" to debate their positions. As the war worsened, protests grew in size and anger. President Johnson was so troubled by events that he did not run in 1968. In 1970, college students were shot at protests in Ohio and Mississippi.

A voice for peace
Folksinger Joan Baez and musicians Pete Seeger, Bob Dylan, and the group Peter, Paul and Mary sang at protests.

Leaders
Famous baby doctor and author Benjamin Spock, far left, marches with civil rights leader Dr. Martin Luther King Jr. at a 5,000-strong antiwar rally in Chicago in 1967. The influence of such well-regarded leaders convinced many Americans to oppose the war.

1969 Moratorium Against the War button

moratorium

Flowers instead of bullets
In one of the most famous photographs of the antiwar movement, a demonstrator places carnations in the barrels of military police rifles. The incident occurred at a 1967 demonstration by more than 100,000 protesters at the Pentagon in Washington, D.C.

Tear gas canister

Tear gas mask

Launcher for tear gas canister

Kent State
Ohio National Guardsmen fire tear gas at Kent State University protestors in May 1970. Troops later killed four students and wounded others—some just students walking to class. Two students at Jackson State College in Mississippi were also killed by police that month.

Fighting back
A protester in Berkeley, California, hurls a tear gas canister back at police who had fired it, in 1970. Tear gas forced most demonstrators to retreat.

US Capitol Building

North Vietnamese flag

Vietnam Veterans Against the War symbol

March for a moratorium on the war
In November 1969, huge demonstrations were held urging a moratorium—a temporary halt in the fighting. One march filled Pennsylvania Avenue, near the Capitol Building in Washington, D.C. Signs called for US troops to get "Out Now" and for the release of jailed antiwar activists. Most protests were peaceful, but clashes with police did occur.

Vietnam veterans against the war
Among the strongest opponents of the conflict were Vietnam veterans, shown here marching in Miami Beach in 1972. Many antiwar veterans threw their medals away in protest.

Silver Star

Dove of peace

McGovern campaign button

Peace candidate
Senator George McGovern of South Dakota ran against Nixon in 1972. McGovern was a World War II pilot and respected in Congress. Yet he could not unify Democrats behind his antiwar message. Nixon won in a landslide.

US withdraws

In 1969, President Nixon pressed for "Vietnamization" of the war. This meant training South Vietnam's military to take on a larger role in the conflict and withdrawing US forces, which numbered 543,000. ARVN soldiers fought well when led by able commanders. Sadly, many of their top officers lacked military ability. It would be years before US troops were replaced. Nixon hoped to limit US casualties, but bloody battles continued, angering soldiers sent into action even as the US was leaving Vietnam.

North Vietnamese flag

RVN flag

A victory
South Vietnamese security forces fighting alongside the ARVN show off a captured North Vietnamese flag. Viet Cong arms and munitions were taken during counterinsurgency operations near the DMZ.

Creighton Abrams
General Abrams took command of MACV in 1968, replacing General Westmoreland. Abrams was ordered to end large-scale US operations and supervise Vietnamization of the war.

Homeward bound
Troops board a Chinook en route to the US. Withdrawal of 25,000 US troops began in June 1969.

General Thi   *President Thieu*

A chest full of medals
South Vietnamese president Thieu awards a medal. He is joined by General Lam Quang Thi. Thieu was criticized as a weak military leader. He and Thi led the Vietnamization effort.

Ngo Guang Truong
ARVN commander General Truong shows captured weapons to US secretary of state William Rogers. Truong was highly regarded.

AVRN troops on patrol
South Vietnamese Marines gather at a village in the Mekong Delta on a mission to cut a VC supply route. As US troops withdrew, ARVN forces assumed more duties. To build a bigger military, South Vietnam began drafting men ages 17 to 43.

Hamburger Hill
On May 10, 1969, heliborne troops attacked NVA forces dug in on Ap Bia Mountain, near the Laos border. The military called this peak Hill 937. A battle raged for 10 days, resulting in 46 US deaths and 400 wounded. Troopers dubbed the mountain "Hamburger Hill," because they felt they had been thrown into a meat grinder. Joined by ARVN troops, they captured Ap Bia, but were ordered to abandon it. Many believed the losses had been for nothing. Hamburger Hill was the last major battle fought by US troops.

Dragon

Leopard

Yellow
Leopard patch

Black
Dragon patch

Patches
South Vietnamese Special Forces wore patches. Yellow Leopards were paratroopers. Black Dragons attacked the Ho Chi Minh Trail.

Reinforcements land
Paratroopers join the battle for Ap Bia. The peak dominated the strategic A Shau Valley, which was a route for VC troops and supplies to the Central Highlands.

Medics aid the wounded
US and ARVN "walking wounded" make their way down Ap Bia Mountain with the help of medics after the fight for Hamburger Hill. Some will be taken to rear units for treatment. Many will be flown out by medevac helicopters. The mildly injured will return to their units.

NVA bases and supply routes

DMZ

Quang Tri
Hué

LAOS

Kontum
Pleiku

CAMBODIA

SOUTH VIETNAM

Central Highlands

An Loc

Tay Ninh

Saigon

Mekong River

N
W—E
S

South China Sea

✳ Battle sites

Areas lost by S. Vietnam in 1972

NVA Eastertide Offensive

Key battles of 1972

The NVA March 30 offensive surprised the ARVN. The invasion triggered struggles at Kontum, Quang Tri, and An Loc. The Communists were defeated by September.

Last air assaults

Through 1970, US forces withdrew, but air support continued. Nixon ordered bombings in Cambodia, and US and ARVN forces struck Communist bases. In 1971, ARVN troops entered Laos, but were routed. By 1972, US offensive operations had ended. Only 70,000 US troops remained. In February, Nixon opened diplomatic talks with Chinese premier Zhou En-lai. In March, Hanoi sent 125,000 troops on the attack. ARVN units fell back until the "Linebacker" air campaign struck strategic targets in the North. ARVN troops pushed back the Communists, ending the "Spring Offensive."

Nixon and Zhou toast

When Nixon visited Beijing, Vietnamese Communists worried he would make a deal to withdraw Chinese support from Hanoi. They opposed any call for peace that would leave Vietnam divided.

Advancing NVA soldiers

Camouflaged NVA troops trudge along a trail in Cambodia, heading for South Vietnam. They are on the way to join the Spring Offensive of early 1972.

Awaiting a lift

South Vietnamese troops near An Loc prepare for helicopter transport in April 1972. An Loc was between the Communists and their objective—Saigon, 75 miles (120 km) away.

Preparing to fire

An NVA soldier loads a shell into a mortar—a favored Communist weapon. Most mortars could be carried by two soldiers, while others carried the ammunition.

James Hollingsworth
General James Hollingsworth planned air attacks at An Loc and advised ARVN corps defending Saigon.

Crewman patch
Named for the site of the Wright brothers' first flight, the USS *Kitty Hawk* was a Navy carrier whose jets helped stem the Communist Spring Offensive.

Wright brothers' plane

500-lb (230-kg) bomb

Loading bombs
Crewmen on the USS *Constellation* load fighter-bombers with 500-lb (230-kg) bombs for the Linebacker campaign. The carrier was one of five Navy "flattops" stationed off Vietnam. The campaign also dropped mines into North Vietnamese harbors to disrupt the supply chain for Hanoi's war effort. It was followed by a second campaign, Linebacker II.

Shark-tooth decoration

Rockets

Cobra helicopter crewman's patch

Cobra helicopter
Cobra attack helicopters such as this Air Cav gunship were among the best weapons in the Linebacker air campaign. The rocket-armed Cobra was an effective tank-destroyer during the Spring Offensive of 1972. More than 200 Soviet-made tanks led the offensive, but they were no match for Cobras.

ARVN counterattack
Tanks of a South Vietnamese armored unit penetrate NVA lines during the ARVN counterthrust at Quang Tri. The Communists could not overcome US command of the air, so ARVN tank crews did not worry about attacks from above. South Vietnamese forces were led by General Ngo Quang Truong, the most capable ARVN general. Truong recaptured Quang Tri Province in a grinding campaign that went through September.

Antitank weapon
The shoulder-fired LAW (light antitank weapon) was key in the ARVN's battle with NVA tanks. Its 66-mm rockets could knock out Soviet-made armor.

Air force patch
In Operation Bullet Shot—the 1972 buildup of US bombers in the Pacific—12,000 personnel and 150 B-52s were at Andersen Air Force Base in Guam. The B-52s flew 3,000 miles (4,800 km) each way to North Vietnam.

The Christmas Bombing
As the 1972 Communist offensive continued, peace talks were under way in Paris. Henry Kissinger headed the US delegation. In October, he announced that an agreement was at hand, and Nixon called off the air campaign. Saigon objected to the treaty, which allowed NVA forces to stay in the South. Talks with Hanoi broke down, and Nixon decided to bomb North Vietnam to demonstrate America's will to come to an agreement. He launched Linebacker II, bombarding North Vietnam from December 18–30. The "Christmas Bombing" was the heaviest of the war and battered the North's industry and transportation system. It brought all parties back to the table to sign a cease-fire.

Identification number

Heroism
Distinguished Flying Cross (DFC) medals are awarded for heroism in flight, in combat or noncombat. Two were awarded in Linebacker II.

Bombs away!
A "string" of 750-lb (340-kg) bombs falls from a B-52D Stratofortress over Vietnam. Air Force and Navy warplanes pounded Hanoi and Haiphong with 20,000 tons (17,850 metric tons) of bombs. The bombing was so massive that the warplanes soon found few remaining targets worth attacking.

Weaving leaves and brush together

70162

B-52 wing patch
The 449th Bombardment Wing flew B-52s in Vietnam. They also flew KC-135s, used for midair refueling.

Black underside for camouflage in night bombing

Antiaircraft defenses
North Vietnamese militia load an antiaircraft gun. The US lost 26 aircraft in Linebacker II, including 15 B-52s. Artillery and MiG fighters shot down three each, SAMs downed 17, and three crashed. By the end, the North's air defenses were destroyed.

US aircraft down
North Vietnamese women salvage parts from the wreckage of an F-111. In Linebacker II, the Air Force lost 20 planes (plus a helicopter); the Navy lost six.

Concealing a bridge

North Vietnamese villagers camouflage a bridge with brush, making it difficult for US warplanes to spot. Air attacks targeted bridges to cut transport links. Camouflage protected small bridges that were essential to the movement of the people. Large bridges, however, were easy targets. The Vietnamese had fought for years against enemies who controlled the air.

Palm leaves

Camouflage

Clearing wood debris

Xuan Thuy

Xuan Thuy joined Ho Chi Minh's Revolutionary Youth League as a teen. The multilingual Thuy became the DRV's chief public negotiator at the Paris Peace Talks. He was a formidable spokesman for Hanoi's top leaders, Le Duan and Le Duc Tho, who were willing to let the talks collapse if terms were unsatisfactory.

Hospital in ruins

Searching for supplies, doctors and nurses pick through the rubble of a Hanoi hospital destroyed by the Christmas Bombing. US airmen tried to avoid hospitals and schools, but high-altitude bombing was not accurate.

Round conference table

Paris Peace Accords

As US air raids hammered North Vietnam in December 1972, Communist delegates to the peace talks agreed to a cease-fire. On January 27, 1973, the United States, North Vietnam, South Vietnam, and the Viet Cong signed the Paris Peace Accords. These provided for a cease-fire and US withdrawal from Vietnam. Vietnamese troops would hold their positions while their leaders consulted on the future. Le Duc Tho and Kissinger were awarded the Nobel Prize for Peace in 1973. Tho declined, however, saying the Accords did not guarantee lasting peace. He was right. Warfare began again in 1975.

Discussing peace terms

Delegates sat at a round table, so no one was "head of the table" and symbolically in charge. A cease-fire was signed on January 27, 1973. Secretary of State William Rogers signed for the US.

Le Duc Tho

Delegates

Henry Kissinger, left, talks with Le Duc Tho through an interpreter, center. The two men led their delegations in the peace talks. Secret negotiations began in 1970. Kissinger created Nixon's Vietnamization policy. Le Duc Tho was determined to reunify Vietnam, even at a high cost to his people.

Madame Binh

Madame Nguyen Thi Binh signs for the National Liberation Front and Viet Cong. She was one of the most important NLF leaders and often seen on American television as the public face of the NLF.

Prisoners of war

More than 660 US servicemen were taken prisoner of war (POW)—a few for nine years. Held in camps in North Vietnam, South Vietnam, Laos, and Cambodia, many were abused. Communist prisoners went to ARVN camps, confining thousands in poor conditions. The treaty called for the release of all POWs once the US left Vietnam. In 1973, Operation Homecoming took US POWs home. Some 1,600 men are still missing in action (MIA).

POW/MIA flag
The National League of POW/MIA Families designed this flag. It is the only flag other than the Stars and Stripes to fly over the White House.

POW/MIA bracelet
As a remembrance, Americans wore silver bracelets inscribed with the names of POWs or MIAs and the dates of their capture or disappearance.

A nurse's comfort
Navy nurse Lt. Patricia Anderson wore a bracelet for Lt. Charles Norris. Upon his release, she helped nurse him back to health.

Nurse Patricia Anderson

Parade of prisoners
American POWs are marched under guard through Hanoi in 1966. Their images were broadcast around the world. US POWs were mostly Air Force and Navy fliers, captured when their planes were shot down. Thirty US POWs managed to escape.

First freedom
American POWs under North Vietnamese guard disembark from a bus on their way to a Hanoi airport in 1973. They will take a flight to freedom, with their first stop in the Philippines. The release was arranged at the Paris talks. Operation Homecoming transported hundreds of POWs back to the US, where they were awarded medals.

POW medal

Communist POWs

There is no accurate count of the thousands of Communist fighters and sympathizers imprisoned during the war. NVA and VC captives went to POW camps in South Vietnam. They were usually interrogated, often brutally—especially if taken by the ARVN. They were classified by rank, fingerprinted, given serial numbers, and photographed. The Accords arranged for POW exchanges between the Communists and US.

Communist star

Hands breaking free from chains

NVA POW medal

Dreary accommodations
American POWs at the "Hanoi Hilton," as they called their prison, have been allowed to talk between bars.

Former NVA POW
The Communists honored their own POWs. Nguyen Huu Thanh, a former US captive, wears the NVA's POW medal.

POW medal

Victory medal

Joyful welcome
Air Force colonel Robert Stirm rushes to embrace his family at Travis Air Force Base, March 1973. He was a POW for more than five years.

A survivor and captive
An NVA soldier of the 304th Division sits, bound and battle-shocked, under the eye of a trooper from the 1st Air Cavalry Division. He was taken during fighting in the Ia Drang Valley, which saw heavy NVA losses.

Binding rope

Taking in suspects
An armed US officer brings in suspected Viet Cong for interrogation. The youthfulness of the captives was typical of many South Vietnamese, who seemed to be farmers, but were actually guerrillas.

The fall of Saigon

Gerald R. Ford
In 1974, Vice President Ford replaced Nixon, who resigned amid scandal. The NVA offensive violated the 1973 Accords, but Ford did not fight it. Congress—and most Americans—were weary of the war.

Van Tien Dung
General Dung had been a top NVA commander since 1953 and had fought at Dien Bien Phu. In 1975, he led the campaign that broke through ARVN defenses in the Central Highlands and charged on to Saigon.

In 1973, Nixon promised to strike if the Communists resumed attacks on South Vietnam. But Congress had cut off funds to aid Saigon. When the NVA invaded Phuoc Long in late 1974, Ford, too, could do nothing. The South Vietnamese were on their own. The final NVA campaign went into full swing in March 1975. Better armed than the ARVN, the NVA swept through South Vietnam, capturing Saigon in April and ending 30 years of fighting.

Looking for safety
ARVN soldiers help villagers cross a footbridge 50 miles (80 km) outside Saigon. Hordes of frightened South Vietnamese left their homes to escape the fighting. Many had no food, water, or shelter, and thousands died. Some soldiers left their units to rejoin their families fleeing the invasion.

The struggle to escape
Desperate Saigon citizens wave identification papers as they try to board a US Embassy bus headed for the airport. Those who worked for the government or the Americans were at risk of punishment by NVA forces.

Last-minute evacuation
A US helicopter loads passengers from a helipad near the US Embassy on April 29, 1975. By April 30, more than 3,000 Americans, South Vietnamese, and other foreign nationals had been evacuated. That day, South Vietnam surrendered. Another 400 people trying to escape were left behind at the embassy.

Final campaign

The NVA offensive of March-April 1975 was named the Ho Chi Minh Campaign. ARVN troops fought hard, even though they were attacked from all sides and had no US air support. The ARVN inflicted heavy casualties on the NVA, but were wiped out in less than two months.

▬ Final NVA campaign March–April 1975
★ South Vietnamese cities and provinces captured by the NVA

Crashing the palace gates

A tank sporting a Viet Cong flag rumbles into the South Vietnamese presidential palace compound on the day of surrender. Until now, infantry and guerrillas had done most of the Communist fighting, but the final offensive was fought by a modern mechanized army. The final assaults were spearheaded by NVA armor.

Victory medal

The Victory Order and Decoration was awarded for fighting South Vietnam, the US, and their allies. It had also been given for fighting the French.

The wake of defeat

Thousands of ARVN soldiers threw away their uniforms and boots as they tried to escape Saigon on April 30. Afraid of being made POWs, they dressed as civilians and tried to mix in with the refugees. This photo was taken by Communists entering the city.

Rejoicing in Hanoi

Marchers carry signs, banners, and pictures of Ho Chi Minh. Military units join the celebration, which marked the end of a century-long struggle for independence.

Aftermath

More than 58,000 Americans died in the war; 153,000 were wounded. One million Vietnamese combatants and four million civilians died. Hundreds of thousands of RVN officials were jailed. The new Socialist Republic of Vietnam was a nation shattered by war. Many tried to escape. Today, the population is about 94 million (from 49 million in 1976)—75 percent of people live in rural areas. Economic growth is a healthy 6 percent.

Nationalist poster
Hanoi became Vietnam's capital. Saigon was renamed Ho Chi Minh City. This 1980 poster shows the dove of peace over a united nation.

Monastery
This Buddhist monk was an ARVN soldier. The current government restricts Buddhism and has taken over Buddhist hospitals and schools. Buddhists believe compassion can heal the country.

Remembering the fallen
Visitors to a cemetery honor fallen NVA soldiers at the Vietnamese New Year by burning incense beside the graves. ARVN cemeteries, however, are usually neglected.

Mothers' medal
The "Hero Mother" medal recognizes the sacrifices of North Vietnam's wartime mothers.

A time of peace
Newlyweds pose before a statue of Ho in Ho Chi Minh City. With 7.3 million inhabitants, it is Vietnam's largest city.

The boat people

As Saigon fell, modern history's largest flight of refugees by sea began. Hundreds of thousands of South Vietnamese "boat people" fled in small, overcrowded vessels. Many drowned. Some families spent their life savings to send their children off in a boat, hoping they could make a new start and help the rest of the family follow later. More than a million refugees from the conflict settled in the US.

Rescued

These boat people have been rescued in the South China Sea. They are mainly former government officials or soldiers and their families. The next waves of refugees would be farmers and laborers seeking a better life.

In Hong Kong harbor

Refugees huddle on a boat in Hong Kong harbor in 1979. That year, 69,000 boat people made the 1,000-mile (1,600-km) trip to Hong Kong. Many were Amerasians—children of Vietnamese women and US soldiers.

Overloaded vessel is dangerously low in water

Vietnam veterans

Allied veterans often faced resentment at home. Many people believed they had lost the war; others thought they had fought in an unjust war. At first, some veterans' groups in the US did not want Vietnam veterans as members. In time, it became clear how well Allied servicemen and women had done their duty, and the veterans were given the respect they had earned. Approximately 2.6 million US personnel served in South Vietnam from January 1960 to March 1973. Almost 1.6 million fought in combat, provided combat support, or were exposed to attack.

Fuse (or trigger)

Land mines

Thousands of mines like this Soviet antitank landmine remain in Vietnam. By 2004, 40,000 Vietnamese had died and thousands more had been injured by uncleared mines.

Veteran's buckle

This belt buckle shows Australian service in the war.

Written in stone

A Vietnam vet touches "The Wall," a memorial in Washington, D.C., bearing the names of US war dead. It opened in 1982.

US veterans

Vietnam veterans parade past saluting spectators during 1993 Veterans Day events at the national Vietnam Veterans Memorial. More than 8.2 million veterans served in the US military during the Vietnam era. They are the largest single group of living veterans from America's wars.

Life goes on

A farmer's elephant lumbers by a rusting tank more than 10 years after the war's end. The modern war machine is useless, but the traditional beast of burden still works in the countryside. Vietnam had an enormous task clearing away ruined military equipment after the conflict.

Did you know?

FASCINATING FACTS

One-third of the top National Liberation Front (NLF) political officers were women. Among the most important was Nguyen Thi Binh, chief NLF representative at the Paris peace talks. Many entered the Vietnamese government after the war.

"Mining" warplanes for metals was profitable. The instruments of a US warplane contained up to $5,000 worth of gold, silver, and platinum.

US soldiers often painted their vehicles with an "Ace Of Death" playing card symbol, considered bad luck in Vietnam. They used it to frighten superstitious Vietnamese.

Death's Head playing card

US soldiers were told to destroy letters they received. So, if a soldier were captured, the enemy would not be able to find out personal information from the letters. Most troops kept their letters, however, and reread them often.

NVA field officers wore no badge of rank. They carried pens to show they were officers. The pen was secured with a string and kept in a shirt pocket.

North Vietnamese officer's pen

In the early 1970s, the ARVN captured so many AK-47 assault rifles from the NVA that they gave away thousands to other Southeast Asian armies.

Documents circulated secretly among Communist commanders and officials in South Vietnam were stamped with coded symbols.

An estimated 50,000 Vietnamese children were fathered by US soldiers. The men returned home, leaving mothers and children behind. These "Amerasians" were discriminated against by the Vietnamese government, which considered them American. Some were adopted in the US; most remained outcasts in Vietnam.

The $8.4 million collected to erect the Vietnam Veterans Memorial included donations from more than 275,000 people.

French author Bernard Fall was the leading authority on the Indochina conflict. US commander William Westmoreland studied his works. A former French soldier, Fall attended college in the US and became a professor at Howard University. His works, such as *Street Without Joy*, chronicled the First Indochina War. He was killed by a mine in Vietnam in 1967.

NVA stamp for official documents

Soldiers on patrol did not use anything with a fragrance, such as soap or cologne. The VC might detect the odor and know they were nearby.

Of the 7,484 US women who served in Vietnam, 6,250 (83.5 percent) were nurses. Ten women from the military died, as did 56 civilians—including missionaries, nurses, and journalists. In one tragedy, 37 civilian women died in a plane crash while escorting Amerasian orphans out of the country in April 1975.

Just as US troops had performers entertain them, NVA and VC troops had their own entertainers. Some performances were given in theater spaces in tunnels.

These girls, seen in Ho Chi Minh City, have Vietnamese mothers and American fathers.

Communist performers entertain North Vietnamese troops.

QUESTIONS AND ANSWERS

Q What is a "flying banana"?

A This was the nickname given to banana-shaped military transport helicopters. The H-21 Shawnee has rotors "in tandem"—at the front and back.

H-21 Shawnee transport helicopter

Montagnards sometimes gave US soldiers friendship bracelets and flutes.

Q Were any Vietnamese ethnic groups US allies?

A Yes, the Montagnards, or "mountaineers," were hostile to lowland Vietnamese. The Hmong mountain people aided the US and became refugees after the war. Many built new lives in the US.

Q What is a flash grenade?

A It is a nonlethal hand grenade. Its flash and bang confuse the enemy, who can then be captured.

Q Who has been Vietnam's worst oppressor?

A China: for 2,000 years, the Vietnamese struggled against Chinese rule. Their first rebellion was in 39CE. The Chinese were driven out but reconquered Vietnam a few years later. Vietnam regained freedom in 939CE.

Q Were the Vietnamese known historically as a warlike people?

A The Vietnamese battled five Chinese invasions after 939CE. They defeated Kublai Khan three times—the last in 1287, routing 300,000 Mongol invaders. China recognized Vietnam's independence in 1427.

Q What is the US K-9 Corps?

A The K-9 (for canine) Corps trains dogs for military duties. German shepherds were used as sentry dogs, to sniff out booby traps, and to find VC tunnels. They were so valuable that enemy mortars targeted dog shelters.

Q What was the "domino theory"?

A The theory was that if South Vietnam fell to the Communists, then other Southeast Asian nations would fall— just as a row of dominoes can knock each other down.

Flash grenade

Q When is the worst weather in Vietnam?

A Monsoon season—in summer or winter—has endless rain. Soldiers' clothing never dried, causing boils, disease, and parasite infections.

Q How educated were US soldiers?

A The average education level of nonofficers was 13 years: one year of college. Among volunteers, 79 percent had a high school diploma.

K-9 unit soldier

Q Where was the fiercest fighting?

A Near the border of North Vietnam and Laos. Fifty-three percent of Americans killed died in four provinces: Quang Tri, Thua Thien, Quang Nam, and Quan Tin.

Q What was the main air force target in the North?

A The Doumer Bridge, which carried trains coming from the north into Hanoi. Freight moving by rail from China and the seaport of Haiphong crossed this bridge.

Q Did Buddhist monks demonstrate?

A Yes, they called for negotiations with the Communists. Monks praying in the streets for peace were oppressed by government troops.

South Vietnamese Buddhist monks are penned in by barbed wire as they demonstrate in the early 1970s.

Timeline

In 1946, Vietnamese Communists in Indochina rose up against the French. This First Indochina War ended in defeat of the US-backed French. Vietnam was divided into the Communist North and capitalist South. For 20 years, the US supported the South. The Second Indochina War—the Vietnam War—cost the lives of 58,000 Americans, 1 million Vietnamese combatants, and 4 million civilians. In 1973, US troops withdrew. South Vietnam fell two years later.

Destroyer USS *Maddox* in Gulf of Tonkin

1945–1946 INDOCHINA STRUGGLE
In August 1945, Japan surrenders in World War II, giving up control of French colonies in Indochina. Vietnamese Communist Ho Chi Minh declares the independent Democratic Republic of Vietnam (DRV). France sends troops. First Indochina War begins.

1950–1953 START OF US ADVISORY PHASE
US Military Assistance Advisory Group (MAAG) is set up to aid the French against the Vietminh, the rebel army. The US helps fund the French. The insurgents win control of the countryside.

North Vietnamese stamp showing divided Vietnam

1954 TWO VIETNAMS
The fall in May 1954 of Dien Bien Phu, a French base in northern Indochina, ends the First Indochina War. Peace terms divide the country temporarily into the Vietminh-controlled DRV in the North and the Republic of Vietnam (RVN) in the South. The Vietnamese are to vote on their form of government.

1955–1963 ARMED REVOLT
In 1955, Ngo Dinh Diem becomes president of South Vietnam, and will not allow a vote. Armed insurrection resumes, with the DRV supporting rebels known as Viet Cong (VC). US military advisers increase to 16,000 by 1963, when the Army of the Republic of Vietnam (ARVN) is defeated at Ap Bac.

1963 ASSASSINATIONS
On November 2, a US-backed military coup in South Vietnam overthrows and assassinates Diem. President John F. Kennedy is assassinated on November 22; he is succeeded by Vice President Lyndon B. Johnson.

1964 GULF OF TONKIN INCIDENT
In August, the US military alleges that North Vietnamese gunboats attacked a US vessel in the Gulf of Tonkin. The Senate passes the Gulf of Tonkin Resolution, giving LBJ broad war powers. Air strikes begin on the North.

1965 DIRECT US INTERVENTION
February–March VC attack US base at Pleiku. The first Marine combat troops are deployed to Vietnam and Operation Rolling Thunder begins. LBJ increases US forces to 33,000 troops.

June–July Battle at Dong Xoai pits US Special Forces, sailors, and South Vietnamese troops against VC guerrillas. LBJ increases US forces to 125,000.

Green beret

Eisenhower, center, welcomes Ngo Dinh Diem, front left, at Washington National Airport, 1957.

August Operation Starlite, first major US ground offensive starts; Operation Market Time attacks enemy seaborne supply routes to South Vietnam.

November Battle of Ia Drang Valley involves Air Cavalry assault, first major engagement by troops carried into battle and resupplied by helicopter. Pentagon calls for 400,000 troops.

1966 AIR AND GROUND WARFARE
January After a pause in bombing North Vietnam (in a failed attempt at negotiations) LBJ resumes air campaign.

March VC and North Vietnamese Army troops attack and destroy US Special Forces base in A Shau Valley.

June Massive US air raids on Hanoi and Haiphong destroy much of North Vietnam's fuel supplies.

August Australian troops win Battle of Long Tan.

September–November Operation Attleboro drives VC forces across Cambodian border.

1967 WAR AND ANTIWAR
January Operation Bolo: air campaign inflicts heavy losses on North Vietnamese; in Operation Cedar Falls, US and ARVN troops attack the VC-controlled "Iron Triangle" near Saigon.

Peace-sign button

February In Operation Junction City, US and ARVN strike enemy bases north of Saigon.

April Major antiwar demonstrations in New York City and San Francisco indicate US public is not fully behind war.

May Secretary of Defense Robert McNamara decides war policy is not working; recommends cutting back on bombing. LBJ unsure of course to follow.

July Marines battle NVA at Con Thien; McNamara visits Saigon, and agrees to add 55,000 troops.

August US bombing campaign against North intensifies.

October Antiwar march by 50,000 on Washington, D.C.; bombing of Hanoi and Haiphong increases.

November–December Battle of DakTo.

1968 DEPTHS OF WAR
January–February Massive NVA-VC offensive during the Buddhist New Year, called Tet. South Vietnam is aflame for weeks before the US and government forces regain control.

President Johnson consults with Secretary of Defense Robert McNamara in February 1968.

January–April Siege of US base at Khe Sanh; Marines fight off determined NVA attacks and hold out until siege is broken. Clark Clifford replaces McNamara as secretary of defense.

March My Lai Massacre: US troops of the American Division kill more than 300 civilians at the RVN hamlet of My Lai. Disheartened by growing opposition to the war, and his health failing, LBJ declares he will not run again for president.

July Phoenix program begins: secret campaign to kill enemy sympathizers allegedly kills 40,000 South Vietnamese.

October Rolling Thunder ends. In Rolling Thunder, more bombs were dropped on North Vietnam than the US used in the Pacific Theater in World War II.

November Richard Nixon is elected president, promising to bring peace with honor.

1969 PEACE DISCUSSIONS
January First meetings held in Paris for peace talks. Marines in Operation Dewey Canyon find enemy supply roads from Laos.

March Operation Menu: Nixon approves secret bombing campaign in Cambodia. Policy of Vietnamization begins.

ARVN troops recapture Citadel at Hué, during Tet Offensive.

May 101st Airborne troops capture Hill 937 in the "Battle of Hamburger Hill," costing 46 US lives. It is soon abandoned.

June Nixon announces withdrawal of 25,000 troops later in the year. Regular troop reductions will continue.

August Henry Kissinger meets with North Vietnamese representative in Paris.

September Ho Chi Minh dies at age 79.

1970 WIDENING WAR
April–May US troops invade Cambodia to attack Communist positions.

May Ohio National Guard fires on antiwar demonstrators at Kent State University, killing four and wounding 10.

June Senate repeals Gulf of Tonkin Resolution.

1971 VIETNAMIZATION
February–April ARVN troops strike in Laos in Operation Lam Son.

November US troops number 139,000, down from a peak of 543,500.

1972 BOMBS SPUR TALKS
February Nixon visits China, meets Mao Zedong and other leaders.

NVA attacks in its 1972 offensive.

March–July NVA opens new offensives.

May–October Nixon orders Operation Linebacker, a massive bombing campaign against North Vietnam.

December Communist negotiators hesitate to make peace, so Operation Linebacker II renews bombing.

1973–1975 COMMUNIST TRIUMPH
January 1973 Paris Peace Accords signed by US, North Vietnam, South Vietnam, and Viet Cong; US military presence in Vietnam ends 60 days later.

August 1974 Nixon resigns in disgrace after the Watergate scandal. Vice President Gerald Ford becomes president and pardons Nixon.

January 1975 North Vietnam resumes military campaign against South Vietnam.

March–April 1975 Communist offensive captures Saigon on April 30. North and South Vietnam are united as the Socialist Republic of Vietnam. Hanoi is the capital.

US troops board a helicopter to return home in 1969.

Find out more

The story of the Indochina conflict is told at museums, libraries, and war memorials. Memorials are places where people can honor those who served. Major memorials are in the United States, Vietnam, Australia, South Korea, and France.

A national tribute

The Vietnam Veterans Memorial in Washington, D.C., honors Americans who served in Vietnam. "The Wall," engraved with the names of the fallen, is the central feature. The memorial is one of the most visited US monuments.

Memorial in Australia

The Australian Vietnam Forces National Memorial in Canberra was dedicated in 1992. Its concrete forms are inspired by ancient sacred sites built of "standing stones."

Vietnam Women's Memorial

This sculpture pays tribute to the women who served. Dedicated in 1993, it shows nurses tending a wounded soldier. One looks upward for help—from a chopper, or a higher power?

Three Servicemen

Frederick Hart designed this 1984 memorial, which portrays soldiers in the field.

A rubbing

Visitors can place paper against a name and create a rubbing. Ceremonies are held at the site on Memorial Day and Veterans Day.

The wall of names

A line of visitors forms under rainy skies at the Vietnam memorial in Washington, D.C., in November 2004. This polished granite wall, designed by architect Maya Lin, holds the names of more than 58,200 US dead and missing. Dedicated in November 1982, the $8.4 million memorial was established by the Vietnam Veterans Memorial Fund, founded by Vietnam veterans.

Memorial in France

The Memorial to the Wars in Indochina honors French veterans. Inaugurated in 1993, it holds the remains of more than 23,000 French—including 3,515 civilians—who died from 1940 to 1954.

Australia's war museum

The Australian War Memorial pays tribute to the dead from all the nation's wars. The museum uses exhibits and research facilities to teach about war.

Tunnel tours

The former VC tunnel complex at Cu Chi is one of Vietnam's most popular tourist attractions. Visitors go into the tunnels to see reconstructed living spaces, including barracks, meeting rooms, and kitchens.

PLACES TO VISIT

NATIONAL MUSEUM OF AMERICAN HISTORY, WASHINGTON, D.C.

"The Price of Freedom: Americans At War" exhibit examines the ways war has shaped US history. It features the Vietnam War.

NATIONAL MUSEUM OF THE US AIR FORCE, DAYTON, OHIO

This is the world's largest military aviation museum. Exhibits include US helicopters and fixed-wing aircraft of the Vietnam War.

NEW YORK VIETNAM VETERANS MEMORIAL, NEW YORK, NEW YORK

Excerpts of letters, diary entries, and poems written by Americans during the war are etched into the Memorial wall. These are supplemented by news dispatches.

VIETNAM-ERA EDUCATION CENTER, NEW JERSEY VIETNAM VETERANS' MEMORIAL, HOLMDEL, NEW JERSEY

The first museum of its kind in the US, the center focuses solely on the Vietnam War. The collection includes photos, timelines, films, letters, and interactive displays.

THE IMPERIAL CITADEL, HUÉ, VIETNAM

The Citadel in Hué was the residence of the Nguyen emperors. Much of the Citadel was reduced to rubble in the Tet Offensive of 1968. Restoration is under way.

THE WEST POINT MUSEUM, WEST POINT, NEW YORK

The galleries interpret the history of the US Army from colonial times to today. Weapons, gear, and art are shown in displays devoted to the Vietnam War. An NVA uniform is shown along with US jungle fatigues.

Learning about the war

Vietnamese schoolchildren take a class trip to view a MiG-21 fighter at a Hanoi military museum. This plane was in the squadron that defended their city against US air raids. The trip is part of a 25th-anniversary celebration of the fall of Saigon.

USEFUL WEBSITES

- Read about The Vietnam Project at Texas Tech University: **star.vietnam.ttu.edu/index.htm**
- View photographs that show a North Vietnamese perspective: **www.anothervietnam.com**
- This National Park Service site details the building of the Vietnam Veterans Memorial: **www.nps.gov/vive**
- Visitors can locate names of service members on The Wall: **www.viewthewall.com**
- View Vietnam War-era artifacts and memorabilia: **www.vietnamwall.org**
- Find photographs and general information about the Vietnam War: **www.vietnampix.com**
- Learn more about the Mobile Riverine Force: **www.mrfa.org**

Glossary

AGENT ORANGE
Toxic chemical used by the US military to kill vegetation. Many Vietnam vets and Vietnamese suffered health problems from Agent Orange. Its name came from the orange stripe on its containers.

AIRBORNE
Soldiers who are trained parachutists, also called paratroopers. In Vietnam, helicopters usually carried these troops into battle.

AIR CAVALRY
The helicopter-borne infantry "Air Cav" was supported by fire from helicopter gunships; many Air Cav troopers were part of former horse cavalry regiments.

AIRMOBILE
Helicopter-borne (heliborne) infantry whose units and tactics were first developed during the Vietnam War.

AK–47 assault rifle

AK-47
Soviet-manufactured Kalashnikov assault rifle that was a favored weapon of the VC and NVA.

APC
Armored personnel carrier—an armor-plated vehicle used for transporting troops or supplies; usually armed with a .50-caliber heavy machine gun.

ARVN
Acronym for the Army of the Republic of (South) Vietnam: the South Vietnamese regular army; pronounced "Arvin."

BASE CAMP
A central resupply base for units in the field; location for headquarters, artillery batteries, and airfields.

BIRD
Soldiers' term for a helicopter or aircraft.

BOAT PEOPLE
South Vietnamese refugees who fled by boat after the Communist victory in 1975. Thousands drowned in the South China Sea. Many were rescued and taken in by neighboring countries and the US.

BODY COUNT
The military's count of the number of enemy troops killed during an operation.

CHARLIE
Nickname for Viet Cong or NVA; taken from "Victor Charlie," radio code for the letters *V* and *C* in messages about the VC.

CHINOOK CH-47
A US cargo helicopter.

CHOPPER
A helicopter. Vietnam was the first "helicopter war."

CLAYMORE
Widely used antipersonnel mine that hurled projectiles up to 300 ft (100 m).

COBRA
AH-1G attack helicopter, armed with rockets and machine guns.

COMPOUND
A fortified US or Allied installation that served as a camp and fortress.

CONCERTINA WIRE
Coiled barbed wire with razor-sharp edges that was laid to protect the perimeter of a fortified position.

COUNTERINSURGENCY
Organized antiguerrilla (anti-insurgent) warfare that armed and trained local militias to defend their communities. Methods included guerrilla tactics of surprise, concealment, and assassination.

C-rations

C-RATIONS
Combat rations, or meals, for use in the field; meals included a canned main course, canned fruit, packets of dessert and coffee, cigarettes, and gum.

DEFOLIATION
Destroying vegetation (foliage) by spraying toxic chemicals such as Agent Orange. It was widely used in Vietnam.

DMZ
The Demilitarized Zone was the dividing line between North and South Vietnam at the 17th parallel. It was to be kept free of military installations or occupation.

DRV
Democratic Republic of Vietnam—the original name given by Ho Chi Minh to Vietnam when he proclaimed independence in 1945. After 1954, the name referred to Communist-dominated North Vietnam, with the capital Hanoi.

Special Forces base camp in the Central Highlands

DUSTOFF
Emergency evacuation of the wounded by a medical helicopter; a medevac.

Dustoff buckle

FIRE BASE
A temporary artillery encampment set up to support ground operations with cannon fire or rockets.

FIREFIGHT
A brief battle, or exchange of fire, with the enemy.

FLAK JACKET
A vest worn for protection from shrapnel—metal hurled by shells, mines, or grenades.

FRIENDLY FIRE
Accidental attacks on US or Allied soldiers by other US or Allied soldiers, aircraft, or artillery—usually the result of being mistaken for the enemy.

Flak jacket

GREEN BERETS
US Special Forces trained in counterinsurgency warfare and for operations behind enemy positions; they wore green berets.

GRUNT
US infantry's ironic term for infantrymen—the lowest in military status.

GUNSHIP
An armed helicopter or fixed-wing aircraft used to support ground troops.

HAMMER AND ANVIL
The tactic of partially encircling an enemy position with one force (the anvil) while other units (the hammer) drive the enemy out of hiding. The hammer attempts to smash the enemy against the anvil.

HANOI HILTON
Name of North Vietnam's Hoa Lo Prison given by Americans held prisoner there; Hiltons are famous luxury hotels.

HUEY
Nickname for the UH-1 helicopters.

IN-COUNTRY
A soldier serving in Vietnam was said to be "in-country."

IRON TRIANGLE
Viet Cong-dominated area between the Thi Tinh and Saigon rivers northwest of Saigon.

LZ
A landing zone for helicopters, usually near the battlefront. LZs often grew into permanent base camps.

M-16
American assault rifle used by US and ARVN troops.

MAAG
Military Assistance Advisory Group.

MACV
Military Assistance Command, Vietnam; it replaced MAAG in 1962.

MEDEVAC
Evacuation of the wounded from the battlefield by helicopter.

MIA
"Missing in Action," the military term for a serviceman or woman whose whereabouts after combat are unknown.

NAM
Soldiers' slang for Vietnam.

NAPALM
A jellied petroleum material that burns fiercely; it is fired from flamethrowers or contained in bombs.

NLF
National Liberation Front, the political wing of the South Vietnamese insurgency fighting the Republic of (South) Vietnam.

NVA
North Vietnamese Army—the regular troops of the DRV.

POW
"Prisoner of War"—a serviceman or woman who has been captured by the enemy.

PUNJI STICKS
Sharpened bamboo stakes set in camouflaged pits.

RANGERS
Elite commandos in the US Army, trained for long-range reconnaissance (scouting) and dangerous combat missions.

RVN
Republic of Vietnam, the name given to South Vietnam when it was established in 1955.

SEABEES
Navy construction engineers who built airfields, bases, and roads swiftly, often under combat conditions. From the letters *CB*, for "construction battalion."

SEALS
Navy personnel who are part of special warfare "Sea, Air, Land" teams.

SEARCH AND DESTROY
Operations in which troops searched an area to find and destroy Communist forces, supply caches, and living quarters.

STRATEGIC HAMLETS
Fortified villages set up by US and ARVN forces to protect locals against attacks from Communist insurgents.

TET
The Buddhist lunar New Year. Thousands of VC guerrillas attacked US and ARVN positions during the Tet holiday in 1968.

Tunnel rat gas mask

TUNNEL RATS
The men who crawled into VC tunnels took this nickname.

VC
Short for Viet Cong, the South Vietnamese Communist guerrillas.

VIETNAMESE POPULAR FORCES
South Vietnamese military units made up of civilians.

VIETNAMIZATION
US policy to turn over the fighting to the South Vietnamese Army; established by President Nixon.

ZIPPO
A flamethrower that shot napalm; named for a type of cigarette lighter. A "Zippo job" was a mission to set Communist-held positions on fire.

Zippo in a firefight

Index

Acknowledgments

DK Publishing, Inc. and Media Projects Inc., offer grateful thanks to: Clifford J. Rogers, Associate Professor of History, United States Military Academy; Steve R. Waddell, Associate Professor of History, United States Military Academy; Erika Rubel; Mark Tolf; David Mager; Michael Harris; Albert Moore; Doug Niven; Tim Page; Emma Naidoo; Jim Messinger; Bob Taylor; Justin Saffell; Ed Emering; Robert W. King; Ngo Vinh Long; Rev. Diedrik Nelson; Margie Ortiz and Terry Adams; Sema at Art-Hanoi; Ronnie Oldham; Jeff Lindsay; Tex Pantaleo; Robert H. Stoner, USNR (Ret.); Ron Toelke for cartography; Rob Stokes for relief mapping; Brian A. Benedict; Madeline Mancini; and Madeline Farbman; Victoria Pyke for proofreading the relaunch version and Helen Peters for indexing it.

Photography and Art Credits
(t=top; b=bottom; l=left; r=right; c=center; a=above)
American Museum of Military History: 33bl. **joelscoins.com**: 7tl. **anothervietnam.com**: © Mai Nam, 21brc; © Tran Phac, 22tl; © Le Minh Truong, 22–23, 25br, 25b, 40–41; © Vo Ann Khanh, 33br; © VNA, 44bl, 56–57tc; © Duong Thanh Phong, 46tl, 60–61. **Art-hanoi. com**: 4crt, 19bc. **Associated Press**: 10bl, 13br, 38–39c, 69tl. **Australian War Memorial**: 69tcl. **Bernie Boston**: 50bl. **Boston University Archives**: 39tr.

brownwater-navy.com: 42cr. **James Burmester**: 4clt, 15bc, 37br, 53cr. **Michael Burr**: 19r, 19bc. **Canadian Forces National Defense Ministry**: 4crb, 63cl. **CORBIS**: 35cr,58bl; © Alinari Archives/CORBIS: 7tr; Bettman/CORBIS: 6cl; 7cr, 8tl, 8tr, 8–9b, 9cl, 9bc, 10tr, 10c, 16bc, 17tc, 17br, 18b, 20br, 21br, 25tl, 31tc, 34bl, 34–35tc, 38tl, 38bl, 38bc, 39cl, 39crt, 40b, 42bl, 43tr, 43cr, 45br, 50cl, 50–51c, 51tl, 51tr, 51cr, 51br, 51b, 54–55, 55tr, 57tr, 57bl, 60bc, 60bl, 63tr; © George Hall/CORBIS: 34br; © Jeremy Horner/CORBIS: 62tl; © Hulton- Deutsch Collection/CORBIS: 21t; © John R. Jones, Papilio/CORBIS: 46cr, 69bcl; © Catherine Karnow/CORBIS: 64bl; © Wally McNamee/CORBIS: 63cr; © Francoise de Mulder/CORBIS: 61tr; © Tim Page/CORBIS: 38cl, 62–63b; © Steve Raymer/CORBIS: 63b; Reuters/CORBIS: 69bl; © Roman Soumar/CORBIS: 46br; CORBIS SYGMA: 6tr; © Darren Whiteside/Reuters/CORBIS: 62bl. **DK Picture Library**: © DK Picture Library: 48tl; © DK Picture Library, courtesy Museum of American Politcal Life/University of Hartford: 51bl (inset); © Philip Blenkinsop/DK Picture Library: 70–71 bkgnd; © DK Picture Library, courtesy of Andrew L. Chernack: 23cl, 26b (scarf, canteen, pouch, oil can), 28cc (NVA knife); © David Mager/DK Picture Library, courtesy Mark Tolf: 2cr, 4tr, 4tc, 11cl, 13cl, 15tr (inset), 27 lower cr, 27 upper c, 27tr, 29t

(M-1 carbine, access.), 29cl (cleaning kit and grenades), 29c (M16 access.), 30bl, 30tl (inset), 30cl, 31tr (inset), 32cl, 32bc, 33cl, 35tr (patches), 37bc, 38tr, 41c (inset), 47 (all equipment), 49bc, 51cr (inset), 55bl, 56cl (medal), 58bc, 65bl, 66cr, 70tr, 71r; © Stephen Oliver/DK Picture Library: 11bc; © Tim Ridley/DK Picture Library, courtesy of the Ministry of Defence Pattern Room, Nottingham: 2tcl, 28bcl (RPG-7 and accessories), 29tcr (M16A1), 29bcr (M79); © Laura Wickenden/DK Picture Library: 46bcl. **Emering Coll.**: 2tr, 9bl (inset), 14tr, 15c (inset), 20tl, 37tc, 37te, 37tcr, 37cr, 37b, 59tc (POW & medal), 61cr, 62cr. **Folio, Inc.** © Rob Crandall: 68l. **Michael Harris**: 62cl. **Getty Images**: Keystone / Hulton Archive 57cl. **Lyndon Baines Johnson Pres. Lib.**: 11br, 15t, 20tl, 24tl, 48cl, 67cl. **John F. Kennedy Pres. Lib.**: 11tr. **Robert W. King**: 21tr. **Coll. Ted Laurenson/©Diggitt McLaughlin**: 4tl, 16tl, 17cl, 50tr, 66br. **LJMilitaria**: 20bc (inset), 55tc, 56tl, 56cl (patch). **John P. Conway/ vhpamuseum.org**: 32tl, 55cr, 71tl. **Library of Congress**: 10–11c, 11cr, 13tr, 14c, 14b, 16tr, 16bl, 16–17b, 17tl, 18cl, 19b, 21cl, 21bl, 23tc, 24b, 24cl, 26cl, 32cl, 39br, 45tc, 45cl, 45cr, 47tl, 49tr, 50tr, 52tr, 53cr, 53tl, 54cl, 55br, 57tc, 57br, 59tr, 60tl, 60cl (UPI), 61br, 66bc. © **Jeff Lindsay**: 65tl. **Mobile Riverine Forces Association/© Dan Dodd**: 34cl, 42c (two patches, inset), 42cr, 43tl, 71b. **MPI Archives**: 2c, 50t, 50c, 59br, 65b. **Andrea Morland**: 68tr. **National Archives**: 2br, 6bl, 8bl, 9tc, 12tl, 14tcl, 15cr, 15bl, 16ca, 16tr, 16–17b, 17tr, 18tl, 19cl, 23tr, 23br, 24tr, 25tr, 25cr, 26–27c, 27tl, 27bl, 27ccr, 28tl, 28tr, 28br, 28cl (grenades),

29br, 32tr, 32br, 32bl, 33bc, 33tr, 35b, 36bl, 36–37, 37tl, 39tc, 40c, 41tr, 41cr, 41br, 43tr, 44tr, 44cr, 44cl, 45tr, 46tcl, 46bl, 49cr, 52b, 53tl, 53tc, 54tr, 55c, 57cr, 60tr, 64–65 bkgnd, 65tr, 66–67 bkgnd, 67b, 70br. **NPS/Terry Allen**: 68b, 68–69 bkgnd. **National Vietnam War Museum**: 34c (inset). **Naval Hist. Soc.**: 12cr, 12–13c. **Rev. Diedrik Nelson**: 9r, 56cl. **Ronnie Max Oldham**: 14cl. **Ngo Vinh Long**: 7cl, 23bc. **Stars and Stripes**: 39tl. **Texas Tech**: 25cl (inset), 29bl, 64tc, 64tr, 67tl, 70l; Anonymous Coll.: 58–59tc, 63tl, 64br; Peter Braestrup Coll.: 49br; Donald Jellema Coll.: 2tl, 28clt, 28bcr, 31cl, 31b, 56br, 64br, 67tr; Douglas Pike Coll.: 13tl, 15cl, 39cr (Cronkite), 48bl, 48cr, 54bl, 56bl; Brig. Gen. Edwin H. Simmons Coll.: 48–49bc. **Tim Page**: 1, 3, 15br, 30tl, 30–31, 31tr, 44–45b, 56bl, 56br, 62t. **Theodore Schweitzer III**: 58cl. **Tribune Media Service**: 38cr. **U.S. Air Force**: 20cl, 21tcr, 34tl, 36tl, 36tr. **U.S. Army**: 17tr, 27crb, 49tl, 52cl, 55tl, 56–57cc. **U.S. Army Ctr for Mil. Hist.**: 6–7bc, 11tl, 52tr (inset), 65tl, 0.S. Army Mil. Hist. Inst.: 65cr. **U.S. Navy**: 12bl, 42tr, 43cl, 58bc (nurse). **U.S. Navy, Naval Hist. Ctr**: 2 clb, 12c (inset), 12–13b, 66tr. **Vietnam Veterans Assoc. of Australia**: 63c. **VietnamWall.org**: 2bl, 2bc, 9tl (inset), 10cl, 25tl (patch), 26ct, 27br, 28bl, 30c, 33cr, 58tl, 58tc (bracelet), 64tl, 65tl (bracelet & flute), 71cl. **www.aceworksbusy. com**: 4bl, 31cla

All other images © Dorling Kindersley

For further information see:
www.dkimages.com